BUILDING FLUENCY WITH READERS THEATRE

RECENT TITLES IN TEACHER IDEAS PRESS' READERS THEATRE SERIES

How and Why Stories for Readers Theatre
Judy Wolfman

Born Storytellers: Readers Theatre Celebrates the Lives and Literature of Classic Authors
Ann N. Black

Around the World Through Holidays: Cross Curricular Readers Theatre
Written and Illustrated by Carol Peterson

Wings of Fancy: Using Readers Theatre to Study Fantasy Genre
Joan Garner

Nonfiction Readers Theatre for Beginning Readers
Anthony D. Fredericks

Mother Goose Readers Theatre for Beginning Readers
Anthony D. Fredericks

MORE Frantic Frogs and Other Frankly Fractured Folktales for Readers Theatre
Anthony D. Fredericks

Songs and Rhymes Readers Theatre for Beginning Readers
Anthony D. Fredericks

Readers Theatre for Middle School Boys: Investigating the Strange and Mysterious
Ann N. Black

African Legends, Myths, and Folktales for Readers Theatre
Anthony D. Fredericks

Against All Odds: Readers Theatre for Grades 3-8
Suzanne I. Barchers and Michael Ruscoe

Readers Theatre for African American History
Jeff Sanders and Nancy I. Sanders

BUILDING FLUENCY WITH READERS THEATRE

Motivational Strategies, Successful Lessons and Dynamic Scripts to Develop Fluency, Comprehension, Writing and Vocabulary

Anthony D. Fredericks

Readers Theatre

Teacher Ideas Press

An imprint of Libraries Unlimited
Westport, Connecticut • London

Library of Congress Cataloging-in-Publication Data

Fredericks, Anthony D.
 Building fluency with readers theatre : motivational strategies, successful lessons and dynamic scripts to develop fluency, comprehension, writing and vocabulary / Anthony D. Fredericks.
  p. cm. — (Readers theatre)
 Includes bibliographical references and index.
 ISBN 978-1-59158-733-0 (alk. paper)
 1. Readers' theater. 2. Drama in education. I. Title.
 PN2081.R4F72 2008
 372.67'6—dc22   2008024083

British Library Cataloguing in Publication Data is available.

Library of Congress Catalog Card Number: 2008024083
ISBN: 978-1-59158-733-0

First published in 2008

Libraries Unlimited/Teacher Ideas Press, 88 Post Road West, Westport, CT 06881
A Member of the Greenwood Publishing Group, Inc.
www.lu.com

Printed in the United States of America

The paper used in this book complies with the
Permanent Paper Standard issued by the National
Information Standards Organization (Z39.48–1984).

10 9 8 7 6 5 4 3 2 1

Contents

Introduction

The air was saturated with moisture and the sun hung overhead like a giant punishing orb as I pulled into the parking lot of Central Elementary School. I had been invited as a visiting children's author to this rural school in South Carolina about nine months earlier. I was truly looking forward to sharing my books, my passion for writing, and my love of children's literature through a series of interactive assemblies and classroom visits. I had also been invited to visit Naomi Britton's fourth-grade classroom that afternoon to see a student-led production of "Don't Kiss Sleeping Beauty: She's Got Really Bad Breath"—a script from my readers theatre book *Frantic Frogs and Other Frankly Fractured Folktales for Readers Theatre* (Westport, CT: Teacher Ideas Press, 1993).

After a full morning of assemblies and writing workshops and an afternoon packed with grade level meetings, reading workshops, and autograph sessions, I eventually found my way to Naomi's classroom. She introduced me to her students and then quickly got them ready to produce the script. I watched enthralled as the "players" delivered a production that would have been worthy of several Academy Awards (I certainly would have given every actor and actress a "Tony!"). The students were actively engaged and well-versed in all their lines and all their roles. The production was both humorous and sincere, practiced and personal. At the end I rose and gave the entire cast a one-man standing ovation. My smile must have been several miles wide as I congratulated every student and celebrated a production that was both magical and dynamic.

As the students were getting ready for dismissal, Naomi pulled me over and told me that all the students in the production had been identified as below-level readers at the start of the school year. Every one of them had approached reading with uneasiness, reluctance, and a hesitation born of several years of literary frustration. She said that all of the students had hated reading at the beginning of the school year simply because they just couldn't see any reason to read. They each came to fourth-grade reading at least two grade levels below expectation, along with an "attitude" that was negative and defiant.

But Naomi had a secret weapon—readers theatre! She had read some of my readers theatre books and investigated several other resources. She knew the power of readers theatre to energize the reading curriculum and promote literacy across the curriculum. But, as she told me, she also saw something else happening with her students. Not only were their attitudes about reading becoming more positive, they were becoming more fluent readers, too. Their pace, delivery, and "comfortableness" with reading were dramatically and positively affected when they had regular opportunities to participate in a range of readers theatre opportunities.

"For me," Naomi stated, "readers theatre was the missing instructional key that enhanced my entire reading program. It gave me a tool that could promote, enhance, and stimulate fluency in a meaningful way. I discovered something that was 8000 percent better than that old fashioned 'round robin reading' and something that my students embraced with passion and desire. Do I teach fluency? You bet! I do it every time my students practice and produce another readers theatre script."

Like Naomi, thousands of teachers across the country are discovering the incredible power and instructional magic that readers theatre can add to any literacy program at the elementary level. They are seeing firsthand how students are becoming more comfortable with their reading, more motivated, and more fluent. As a result of readers theatre, students' reading has the capacity to be effortless, smooth, and graceful. More important, students comprehend more of what they read and enjoy the reading experience as never before. To quote Naomi again, "Readers theatre is a tool that will promote, enhance, and stimulate fluency in meaningful ways."

As I travel to other schools and talk with other teachers, I am often asked about the best way to teach and promote fluency. An examination of current textbooks on reading instruction or a survey of popular resource books available for classroom teachers reveals a dearth of instructional information about fluency and how it can be enhanced. That's not surprising. Fluency is not a new concept, but it has received a disproportionate amount of attention in basal reading series, teacher preservice training, and popular resources.

Building Reading Fluency with Readers Theatre was written to help you help your students achieve reading fluency success with a proven and motivational teaching technique. It is my hope that you will find within these pages a wealth of dramatic and exciting teaching tools that will reinvigorate your reading program, stimulate your students to new levels of literacy growth, and infect your classroom with spirit, enthusiasm, and excitement!

I hope you're ready for an incredible ride . . . and an equally incredible teaching experience. If so, then hop on board!

Tony Fredericks

PART I

FLUENCY AND READERS THEATRE

CHAPTER 1

Let's Take a Look at Reading Fluency

When I was young I wanted to learn how to ride a bicycle more than anything else in the world. At that time my mother had a really old bicycle that was heavy, creaky, and slow. But, that didn't matter to me. I wanted to learn how to ride, and I figured that any bicycle was better than no bicycle.

To this day I can still conjure up mental images of me in our backyard in Los Angeles trying to master the art of bicycle riding. I would get up on the seat, place my feet on the pedals, and then unceremoniously fall to the ground. I'd climb up once again, get myself positioned in the seat, my feet firmly on the handlebars, and just as I was about to swing my feet onto the pedals I would, once again, fall over on the grass. Again, I would right the bike, position my feet on either side of the frame, place my hands firmly on the grips, place one foot on one pedal, the other foot on the other pedal, and pump like crazy. I would travel for a few feet and then, as before, would lose my balance and fall onto the turf.

Day after day I would try to master the art of bicycle riding. Once in a while my father would come out to hold the handlebars as I climbed up onto the seat and tried to pedal fast enough to overcome inertia and keep myself in an upright position long enough to get to the other side of the yard. Again and again I would get 10 feet, 20 feet, or 30 feet before Newton's Second Law would intervene and I would fall off the bike. But I was determined (perhaps even hard-headed) to learn how to master that clumsy old bicycle.

Finally, after several weeks of demonstrating a basic law of gravity to my younger sisters (boy on nonmoving bicycle will tend to fall over), I slowly began to master the art of bicycle riding. I could maintain my balance, I could keep the pedals moving at a decent rate, I could hold firmly on to the handlebars, and I could keep the bike moving in a forward direction. I discovered that the more I practiced, the more I was able to do all these tasks with a certain degree of automaticity. That is, I could do all the collective tasks in a coordinated fashion without having to think about each one individually. For me, bicycle riding was the ability to seamlessly integrate many skills into a purposeful (and injury-free) journey from point A (front of yard) to point B (back of yard).

Today I can ride a bicycle without even considering all the various skills that concerned me as a child. I can ride my bike for 20, 30, or 50 miles on a summer day enjoying the scenery around me, the countryside in the rural area where I live, and the occasional herd of cows observing me with their typical bovine stares. I don't have to think about the laws of physics that plagued me as a beginning bicycle rider more than 50 years ago. Now bicycle riding is smooth and efficient. I am a fluent rider!

Reading fluency is a lot like bicycle riding fluency. For the moment, let's take a look at what it means to be a "fluent" bicycle rider. Fluent bicycle riders:

- Can pedal the bicycle and hold on to the handlebars at the same time.

- Can keep the bicycle moving in a forward direction at a sufficient speed

- Can maintain their balance without undue compensation.

- Can steer the bicycle in a straight line (or around curves, if necessary).

- Can anticipate dips, bumps, and other road hazards and take the proper course of action to deal with them.

Yes, bicycle riding is a lot like reading. When we read we need to maintain an appropriate course of action, be aware of the details in a selection of text, maintain our attention, and keep focused on the task at hand. When we are able to do all of those tasks in a coordinated fashion, then we are considered to be fluent readers. So, too, when we are able to coordinate a variety of physical tasks and maintain smooth progress down the street are we considered to be fluent bicycle riders.

FLUENCY: A DEFINITION

According to *A Dictionary of Reading and Related Terms* (Harris & Hodges 1995), fluency is "the ability to read smoothly, easily, and readily with freedom from word recognition problems." This implies that when students are able to decode print accurately and effortlessly, they are able to concentrate on the ultimate goal of reading text: comprehension. For this reason, getting meaning from text (e.g., comprehension) is directly related to fluency. In short, fluent readers are those who understand more of what they read.

Some researchers have referred to fluency as the missing ingredient in reading programs (Allington 1983). More important, the report of the National Reading Panel (2000) indicated that fluency should be a key component of effective literacy instruction.

Fluent readers are those who are able to decode and recognize words automatically while reading accurately, quickly, and smoothly—all with the right intonation and expression (Worthy 2005). Fluency is not just about sounding good when reading aloud, but implies that the reader is comfortable with the complexity of the material and equally comfortable with his or her ability to comprehend and interpret that material. Fluent reading takes concentration, thought, and effort; a fluent reader is a practiced reader—someone who has had multiple exposures to text and multiple opportunities to share that text in an expressive manner.

According to Tim Rasinski (2003), reading fluency is the ability to read quickly, effortlessly, and efficiently with good, meaningful expression. Rasinski explains that fluency means much more than mere accuracy in reading. Although many readers can decode words accurately, they may not be fluent (or automatic) in their word recognition. These readers tend to expend a lot of mental energy on figuring out the pronunciation of unknown words, energy that takes away from the more important task of getting to the text's overall meaning: comprehension. As a result, a lack of fluency is often associated with poor comprehension.

Blevins (2001) states that fluent reading is a major goal of reading instruction because decoding print accurately and effortlessly enables students to read for meaning. He further states that students who decode words effortlessly can focus more of their conscious attention on making meaning from text. Fluent readers are those who

1. **read at a rapid rate** (pace—the speed at which oral or silent reading occurs);

2. **automatically recognize words** (smoothness/accuracy—efficient decoding skills); and

3. **phrase correctly** (prosody—the ability to read a text orally using appropriate pitch, stress, and phrasing).

The following chart outlines the behaviors seen in fluent readers as well as those behaviors indicative of nonfluent readers. These reading behaviors are irrespective of grade level.

Fluent Readers	Nonfluent Readers
• Read with expression • Read smoothly and easily • Read at a rapid rate • Read orally with appropriate phrasing • Can recognize many words quickly and accurately • Can read aloud and retell a story accurately • Demonstrate efficient decoding skills • Demonstrate reading comprehension abilities equivalent to their instructional level	• Read mechanically (with little or no expression) • Read at a slow, halting pace • Read with poor phrasing • Read with inadequate intonation • Read word by word • Demonstrate weak word recognition skills • Spend excessive time trying to identify unfamiliar words • Devote insufficient time to comprehension

FLUENT READING: A RUBRIC

Chapter 3 of this book is devoted to the assessment of reading fluency. In addition to the reading passages and scoring criteria promoted in that chapter, you may also find the rubric in figure 1.1 (p. 6) a useful tool in assessing the fluency of selected students in your class. The reading passages in chapter 3 are designed to be used at three separate times during the school year: fall, winter, and spring, to gauge the fluency progress (through the year) of individual students. The rubric in figure 1.1 outlines specific criteria for fluency development that can be assessed at any time during the course of the academic year. Not only does this rubric provide necessary elements of reading fluency, it also provides you with insights on individual students as they progress through your classroom reading program.

Figure 1.1. Reading Fluency Rubric

Name: _____ **Date:** _____

When reading grade level materials, the student reads:	All the time	Most of the time	Some of the time	Never
1. with good pacing	5	3	1	0
2. smoothly	5	3	1	0
3. accurately	5	3	1	0
4. with appropriate phrasing	5	3	1	0
5. with appropriate timing	5	3	1	0
6. with expression	5	3	1	0
7. with appropriate intonation	5	3	1	0
8. with enthusiasm	5	3	1	0
9. with word recognition	5	3	1	0
10. with comprehension	5	3	1	0

TOTAL SCORE:_____

Interpretation:

45–50	Student is a fluent reader
40–45	Student is approaching fluency
30–40	Student needs sustained fluency instruction
Below 30	Student is a nonfluent reader

TEACHER BEHAVIORS THAT CONTRIBUTE TO READING FLUENCY

Reading fluency doesn't just happen. It is the result of a coordinated and systematic mastery of various skills. (Remember how yours truly learned to ride a bicycle?) We know from decades of research that reading fluency is promoted, enhanced, and supported by the actions of classroom teachers. That is to say, what teachers do and practice in a classroom reading program will have a significant and sustained impact on students' development of reading fluency. It is not just the skills or strategies that we teach, it is also the philosophy and beliefs we integrate into our reading program that have a positive impact on students' fluency growth and development.

The teacher behaviors covered in the form in figure 1.2 (p. 8) have been shown to have a positive and profound impact on the fluency development of students. Use this list as a self-evaluation by placing a check mark in front of those behaviors that are a regular element of your instructional practices. Which of these behaviors do you practice every day or several times in an instructional day?

It should be pointed out that reading fluency does not develop overnight. It is part of a long-term effort by teachers to model what good readers do when they read. Ultimately, students' exposure to lots of positive and engaging reading models will be the ultimate determinant in the success they enjoy as fluent and accomplished readers.

REASONS FOR NONFLUENT READING

There are many reasons students fail to read fluently. Allington (1983) offers the following:

- **Lack of Exposure.** Many children have not been exposed to fluent reading models. They may not have seen or heard adults read to them, they may not have parents who value bedtime stories, or they may come from classrooms in which more time was assigned to standardized test preparation than to read-alouds. Children who come from homes in which there are few books or in which adults do not value reading as a family activity may also exhibit nonfluent reading behaviors. Fluent readers are most typically those who have been exposed to and surrounded by positive reading models throughout their lives.

- **The Good-Reader Syndrome.** In most classrooms it is not unusual for good readers to get considerably more attention than poor readers. Good readers receive more attention than do poor readers, and good readers receive more praise than do poor readers (conversely, poor readers get more negative comments than do good readers). Good readers get more positive comments relating to the context or "wholeness" of a reading passage; poor readers often get negative comments focused on individual words or phonemic elements.

- **Lack of Practice Time.** In traditional classrooms good readers tend to spend more time in actual reading activities. These may include reading whole books or complete magazine articles. As assignments are completed (and they may frequently be completed early), good readers are encouraged to spend time in realistic reading endeavors. Poor readers, who may typically struggle with classroom assignments, have few opportunities to read independently. The hidden message to students may be that good readers are those who are offered authentic reading opportunities, while poor readers are those undeserving of such opportunities. The result may be a self-fulfilling prophecy about the role of reading in one's life.

Figure 1.2. Teacher Self-Evaluation on Reading Fluency

I engage in the following classroom activities on a regular (or daily) basis:

_____ reading aloud from a variety of genres

_____ reading aloud with expression

_____ reading aloud with enthusiasm

_____ providing students with multiple opportunities to talk about books

_____ providing students with a model of what good readers do

_____ building on students' home language

_____ filling the classroom with a variety of reading materials

_____ integrating oral reading experiences into every subject area

_____ providing students with opportunities to listen to fluent readers
(e.g., guest speakers, recorded books, etc.)

_____ providing opportunities for students to share reading materials with each
other

From *Building Fluency with Readers Theatre: Motivational Strategies, Successful Lessons and Dynamic Scripts to Develop Fluency, Comprehension, Writing, and Vocabulary* by Anthony D. Fredericks. Westport, CT: Teacher Ideas Press. Copyright © 2008.

- **Frustration.** Poor readers struggle because much of their reading material is at their frustration level. At that level they may tend to read word-by-word, stop and restart several times, or focus on the phonemic elements of individual words. They may not have sufficient opportunities to read material that is at their independent level, that is, material at which they can demonstrate smooth reading behaviors. Good readers, on the other hand, typically spend considerably more time reading at their independent and instructional reading levels. As a result, they have more opportunities to enhance their reading fluency.

- **Missing the "Why" of Reading.** One of the perceptions that poor readers have when asked to define what good readers do is that accomplished readers are able to read words accurately. Good readers, on the other hand, define the act of reading as an interactive process—one in which the central goal is to gain meaning from text. Poor readers define reading in smaller "chunks" (e.g., letters, words) than do good readers. This limited definition also restricts the value of fluency in poor readers' overall interpretation of reading.

FLUENCY: A FINAL THOUGHT

Some teachers equate fluency with speed reading. Not so! Reading quickly is not necessarily synonymous with efficient reading. Plowing through a string of words may be indicative of word recognition mastery, but may not illustrate one's ability to comprehend the overall meaning of those words. Reading fluency is much, much more than simple speed reading. It is reading that is fluid, accurate, and automatic. Most important, it is reading with comprehension. As Regie Routman reminds us, "fluency without comprehension is not reading, it is calling words" (2003).

Fluent reading is practiced reading. It is effortless and engaged. It is reading that is enthusiastic and purposeful. Fluency comes about because students have been exposed to good models as well as sustained opportunities to practice reading in meaningful situations. Like riding a bicycle, fluent reading is part of a process that ensures a comfortable journey with an array of pleasurable vistas along the way.

CHAPTER 2

Instructional Methods to Develop Fluency

It is probably safe to say that reading fluency doesn't just happen! As teachers, we can't hope that students will become fluent just because they have experienced a wide and varied reading curriculum, listened to lots of books, or participated in a literature-rich language arts program. Fluency is not a by-product of a reading program; it is, and should be, a goal of every reading program—a goal that must be planned, taught, and evaluated.

Few reading basal series focus on fluency as an important goal of the reading curriculum. Few of us had college textbooks or college courses that underscored the significance of fluency instruction as a viable element in any child's reading development. But as we saw in the previous chapter, fluency is critical to each child's success in, and appreciation of, reading.

What follows are some of the instructional practices and strategies teachers can use to promote and enhance fluency development. Several of these are probably already in place in your reading instructional plans. Others are offered for your consideration in assisting students in becoming engaged and active participants in all aspects of your reading curriculum.

READING ALOUD

Stimulating imaginations, enhancing listening skills, and introducing students to a variety of literature can all be facilitated when you read aloud to students, particularly when this sharing activity is made a regular and featured part of your instructional plans. Children of all ages enjoy listening to someone read aloud from a new or familiar book. Reading aloud makes language active, stimulating creativity, developing an appreciation for the wide variety of literature that children can begin reading on their own, assisting children in the development of vivid mental pictures, and promoting an easy and natural enjoyment of stories.

Just as important, reading aloud provides children with a positive role model—you! Irrespective of their reading ability, students need fluent, practiced models of reading—models they can emulate and enjoy. By modeling good reading, you provide your students with an example of proficient and fluent reading on a regular basis. They see (and hear) what a fluent reader does with a story—the "smoothness" of dialogue, the correct pacing, the energy and emotion injected into words and phrases, and the power of a story well told.

There are many benefits associated with the read-aloud experience, including the following:

- Reading aloud stimulates children's interest in books and literature. Old "classics" as well as new tales broaden students' exposure to a variety of literature.

- Reading aloud helps students understand that the interpretation of words is just as important as the reading of those words. In short, we read for meaning. This is one of the key elements of fluency.

- Students' reading and subject-area interests are broadened and enlarged when teachers and librarians utilize read-aloud literature from several areas.

- Students are introduced to the patterns of language, including sentence structure, sequence, and the development of story themes.

- Children are provided access to books that may be beyond their independent reading level. As a result, they get to hear what an accomplished reader does with material that they may not necessarily be exposed to in their regular reading program.

- Reading aloud fosters positive attitudes about books and about reading in general.

- Reading aloud helps develop a community of learners within the classroom or library.

- Reading books from many different sources helps children expand their backgrounds of experience, an important element in comprehension development.

- When teachers and librarians read books to their students, they are serving as positive reading models. Students see the pleasure, enjoyment, and excitement of reading demonstrated by an accomplished reader.

- Reading aloud enhances the development of appreciative, comprehensive, and critical listening skills in a variety of informal contexts.

- Reading aloud stimulates children's imaginations, develops their minds, and increases intelligence.

- Reading aloud provides a host of pleasurable sharing experiences and facilitates teacher–student communication.

- Reading aloud helps promote reading as a lifelong activity.

Following are some guidelines you should consider to make the read-aloud experience enjoyable and gratifying for both you and your students:

Making Read-Aloud Successful

1. Take time to read the book before reading it to your students. This will give you a sense of the story necessary for an effective reading.

2. Select a book that both you and the students will enjoy.

3. Occasionally provide opportunities for students to select the literature to be read.

4. Make reading aloud a daily part of your overall instructional program—no matter what grade you teach! When possible, include more than one read-aloud session each day. Consider the beginning of the school day, immediately after a recess or gym period, after lunch, or just before students are dismissed at the end of the day.

5. Sit so that you are positioned in front of the children. This allows for appropriate voice projection and permits all youngsters an opportunity to listen. Also, if you wish to show illustrations in the book, everyone will be able to see them.

6. Emphasize that read-aloud time is solely for the purpose of listening to a book being read aloud. It should not be an opportunity to talk, interrupt, or fidget. Establish a set of "Read-Aloud Rules" and adhere to them.

7. Practice reading with expression. Give different voices to each of the characters, highlight dramatic points in the plot through voice inflection, and speed up or slow down the reading depending on the action. Dramatic readings (when appropriate) draw listeners into the "action" of a book.

8. Be cognizant of the pace of your reading. Provide opportunities for youngsters to create "pictures" in their minds (e.g., mental imagery). It may be necessary to "slow down" your reading to allow children to develop appropriate images.

9. Provide frequent opportunities for youngsters to engage in directed comprehension strategies. It is not necessary to do this for every read-aloud book, but reading aloud can easily and naturally segue into appropriate comprehension opportunities.

10. Begin your read-aloud sessions with short stories and books and gradually progress to longer readings. Be mindful of your students' attention spans and adjust the reading time accordingly.

11. Be sure to expose youngsters to a wide variety of books. Throughout the year, select books from all of the genres of children's literature.

12. Provide opportunities for students to respond to what they have just heard. Discussions are appropriate ways to help students think deeply and critically about any story or book. This is not, however, a time for assessment, but rather a time to pose open-ended questions that expand students' appreciation for a story and encourage reactions to its overall presentation. Here are some appropriate questions you might ask:

    – What did you enjoy most about this story?

    – What did you enjoy the least?

    – What did you enjoy most about the main character?

    – How was the main character similar to or different from you?

    – If you could change anything about the story, what would it be?

    – What would you like to say to the author?

    – What would you tell a friend about this book?

    – How would you change the ending of this story?

Reading aloud can and should be a natural element in your classroom reading program. With regular exposure to the best in children's literature, students quickly get a sense that reading is filled with an abundance of intriguing concepts and fascinating perspectives about the world around them. Read-alouds provide learning opportunities that can magically expand and extend the elementary curriculum in a hundred different ways. In short, reading aloud brings life to reading and reading to life!

READING ALOUD (PART II)

As discussed in the previous section, reading aloud can and should be a regular element of not only your overall reading curriculum, but your entire instructional program. In addition to all the benefits listed in the box, it has been proven by researchers (Cohen 1968; Cunningham & Stanovich 1998; Rasinski 2003) to have a direct impact on students' vocabulary, comprehension, and fluency development.

We have also seen how reading aloud helps students listen to good models of reading. This modeling is critical to the success children experience throughout every aspect of the reading program. But in order for that modeling to be most effective—particularly in terms of fluency development—it must be systematically illustrated for children. That is to say, children must be provided with instruction that draws their attention to the modeling process and its relationship to their own reading progress.

This can be accomplished when you engage your students in selected metacognitive prompts. Notify them orally of what you are attempting to do or what you are thinking about during a read-aloud session. These "mental prompts" alert students to the thoughts accomplished readers consider when they read with fluency. They serve as models for the thinking that students can engage in as they read their own self-selected materials.

To effectively model "fluency in action," select a reading selection and begin to "think out loud," verbalizing what is going on inside your head as you read. Since students cannot observe the thinking process firsthand, the verbalization allows them to get a sense of good thinking as practiced by an accomplished reader. You serve as a most significant role model for students in all their academic endeavors, so "talking to yourself" gives them some firsthand experiences with reading as a thinking process, experiences they can begin to incorporate into their reading practices.

Begin the process by reading aloud a book or story to students, stopping at selected points, and verbalizing the thought processes you are using during the read-aloud. This verbalization is essential, because it provides a viable model for students to copy. Here are some examples:

❖ "As I read this next paragraph, I'm going to read it as though I'm talking with a close friend. I'm going to pretend that we are having a comfortable conversation at a restaurant over a cup of coffee."

❖ "This next passage has a lot of emotion. So I'm going to read it with great feeling. I'm going to read the first part in a very happy voice. Later I'll need to change my voice and read it in a cautious voice."

❖ "I read this section to myself first because I wanted to get a picture in my head of the lake and the grove of trees near the river. Now I will read this part out loud in a smooth and easy way so that I can set up that very important scene for my listeners."

❖ "I want my listeners to feel the power of these words. So, I will read them with lots of energy and excitement. I want them to feel the terror that is beginning to creep into Jeremy's mind."

❖ "This next part of the book is very interesting. So, I will read it in a smooth and deliberate way. I want my listeners to stay with me during this part, so I will read it aloud in an easy, comfortable way."

As you read and model, allow students opportunities to interject their thoughts about what may be going on in their heads as they listen to the selection. Your goal, obviously, will be to have students internalize these processes and be able to do them on their own in all kinds of reading material. Here are some alternate approaches:

- **Partner pairs**. Have students practice the procedure above with a partner. One student reads a passage out loud to another and verbalizes some of the thinking taking place in his or her head. The partner records those thought processes and discusses them with the reader upon completion of the story.

- **Hear this**. Students read a passage into a tape recorder. Afterward, a student plays the recording and stops at selected points to tell a partner or you about some of the thinking that was taking place in his or her head as he or she dealt with the text at that spot.

- **The more the merrier**. Bring other adults into the classroom to model their thinking behavior as they read. The principal, secretary, custodian, librarian, superintendent, and other school-related personnel may all be held up to students as positive reading models. Be sure to provide a brief in-service on the appropriate thinking processes prior to each presentation.

- **Higher and higher**. Invite students from grades higher than yours to visit the classroom and read selected passages to your students. Ask them to model their thinking as they read.

- **Reader of the day**. Designate a student "Reader of the Day," who selects a passage to share with other students and demonstrates the appropriate "think-aloud" procedures. This daily event designates every student as a model for all the other students and validates the utility of think-alouds for all readers in all types of materials.

REPEATED READINGS

One of the most researched strategies for improving students' reading fluency is repeated readings. Initially developed by Jay Samuels (1979), this strategy has long been recognized as an excellent way to help students achieve levels of fluency commensurate with their reading instructional levels. In fact, several researchers (Dowhower 1989; Morgan & Lyon 1979; Martinez & Roser 1985) have concluded that "repeated readings" method helps students

- improve their reading comprehension of unfamiliar passages,

- remember higher-level important information in text,

- engage in greater word recognition accuracy,

- break away from word-by-word reading, and

- enhance fluency development in accordance with grade-level expectations.

In its simplest terms, repeated readings is exactly what it sounds like—students reading a selected passage over and over again until they achieve an appropriate level of proficiency. The underlying concept is that if a student practices enough times with a single piece of text, he or she will begin to demonstrate a level of comfort that translates into smoother reading (fluency), understanding (comprehension), and word recognition. It is important to note, however, that repeated readings achieves its greatest potency with struggling readers, not necessarily with readers who are at grade level or those reading above grade level.

That said, following is an instructional sequence you may wish to use to introduce this most effective teaching strategy to your students. As with any strategy, feel free to modify or alter this in accordance with the dictates of your own classroom reading program, available time, and the individual needs of your students.

Suggested Guidelines for Repeated Readings

1. Identify students who would benefit most from repeated readings (e.g., students struggling with grade level materials).

2. Set aside 10–20 minutes per day for instruction.

3. Select several reading passages to share with a student. These passages should be at the student's instructional reading level (word recognition 90–95 percent). The passages can come from basal reading materials, trade books, textbooks, or other commercial materials. Each passage should be between 100 and 400 words long.

4. Provide the child with one copy of the passage and retain a second copy for yourself.

5. Sit with the child in a quiet area of the classroom.

6. Tell the child that you will read the selected passage through from start to finish. Invite the child to listen carefully to each word, phrase, and sentence as you read it. If necessary, the child may follow along with his or her finger or some other pointer.

7. Invite the child to read the passage orally from start to finish. Note any errors the child makes and re-read the passage orally to the child if he or she makes an excessive number of errors (you may also elect to choose another passage written at a lower level).

8. Encourage the child to orally practice the passage several times until he or she has achieved a reading rate indicated in the chart below:

Grade Level	Correct Words per Minute*
first (second half of year)	50–70
second	80–95
third	95–105
fourth	105–115
fifth	115–135
sixth	135–150

   *modified and adapted from Rasinski (2003)

9. As the student achieves the appropriate level of proficiency indicated in the chart, provide him or her with additional passages at the same or a slightly more difficult reading level.

10. Periodically assess the student (see chapter 3) and record his or her progress. Continue this instructional sequence for a period of approximately five to six weeks.

A few words of caution are in order here. Although the repeated readings technique has been shown to have many positive benefits for students, it does have some limitations, which should not deter you from using this reading strategy, but which you will need to consider in terms of your overall reading curriculum. A few of those considerations are listed below:

- Repeated readings works best with students who are reading below grade level. It has limited impact for students reading on or above grade level.

- Repeated readings should be used judiciously in your classroom reading program. Because students are performing the same task over and over (repeated readings), they will tend to lose attention and become bored. Repeated readings works best when it is used as a short-term, not a long-term, intervention strategy.

- Although it does have a significant impact on students' comprehension development, repeated readings should not be the only strategy used. Comprehension instruction achieves its greatest potency when it is explicitly taught. That is, students must receive direct instruction in the reading strategies that will lead to improved levels of comprehension (Fredericks 2001).

- With its emphasis on accuracy and speed, students may get the mistaken impression that reading is simply an exercise in word recognition improvement in tandem with an increase in reading rate. Students need to know that fluency is just one aspect of a successful reader, not the only one.

I'm sure you will discover, as I have, that repeated readings offers some easy-to-implement opportunities that will enhance the fluency development of your students. If used in a judicious and appropriate manner, it can have a positive impact on the overall reading growth of youngsters.

ORAL SUPPORT READING

Depending on the nature of your classroom reading program, as well as the individual instructional needs of your students, you may consider a variety of effective oral reading techniques designed to improve the reading fluency of youngsters. These strategies can be used with most types of reading material, from basal textbooks to magazines to trade books. You may elect to select the appropriate materials (in accordance with the reading proficiency of selected students), or you may wish to invite students to select the materials used in one or more of the instructional techniques discussed below.

Echo Reading

In this modification of repeated readings, you read a sentence (from a selected text) to a single student sitting next to you. The student repeats the sentence you read. Then you read another sentence, and the student repeats it as before. The advantage of this approach is that the student gets to hear an appropriate model before reading a brief selection on his or her own. In short, the student has the opportunity to hear fluent reading in action.

Choral Reading

This may be one of the most popular and certainly most used literacy activities in any elementary classroom. Simply stated, several students (often an entire class) read together in unison. A classroom full of kids reciting the pledge of allegiance, singing a favorite song together right after recess, or sharing a familiar Mother Goose rhyme as part of a lesson on phonemic awareness are all examples of choral reading (and fluency) in action. Most important, choral reading offers struggling readers a comfortable support system in which all students are working together to ensure a practiced and comfortable presentation. This support system underscores the importance of fluency as a significant skill in all types of literacy activities.

Here are some of the modifications and presentation possibilities for choral reading for your classroom:

Teacher/student reading. This modification takes a little extra effort to be successful. It requires two people reading the same passage out loud in unison. As you are reading a passage (somewhat slower than normal), a single student is also reading right along with you. It is important that the student "match" his or her rate with yours for maximum benefit.

Student/student reading. In this example another student takes over the role of the teacher in the modification above.

Group by group reading. Divide your class into several groups (e.g., row 1, row 2, row 3; boys/girls). One group reads a section of text, then another groups read a successive section of text, and so on.

Student to group reading. In this variation, one student reads one or two lines of a selected piece of text, and then the rest of the class chimes in with a chorus or refrain.

Group to student reading. A large group reads a selected portion of a text, and then one student recites a refrain or chorus. This is repeated throughout a text.

Singing. One of the most natural ways to illustrate the importance of fluency to children is to engage them in a variety of singing activities. Working in concert with your school's music teacher, invite students to learn new songs and sing them together on a regular basis. Point out that when they sing together, they are demonstrating skills similar to reading together.

Songs without music. After students have learned how to sing a song in unison, invite them to read the lyrics of the song together—as a choral group—but without the music.

Books on Tape

This technique provides students with audio support for their repeated readings. Students listen to a book that has been recorded on audiotape. They listen to the recording several times and then read along with the narrator on the fourth or fifth playback of the book. For this to be successful, each book should be recorded at a rate somewhat slower than usual (but with the same inflections and intonations as "normal" reading) to allow students to maintain the same pace as the reader.

I have found that recorded books are excellent adjuncts to any classroom reading program—irrespective of the varied reading levels students may exhibit. They are perhaps the ideal way for students to listen to fluent readers in action. Students hear the passion, intonation, excitement, and pacing of an accomplished reader (or several readers) over a wide range of reading materials.

The best books on tape are those you record yourself! As a former reading specialist, I discovered many commercial enterprises with loads of audio books or "classics on tape" for remedial readers. The problem with most of these professionally produced tapes was that the readers read at rates that were not necessarily consistent with the reading rates (and fluency levels) of my students. Also, the inclusion of musical backgrounds and sound effects made the tapes commercially viable, but less than appropriate for promoting appropriate fluency development in a classroom setting.

Consequently, the best books-on-tape program was the one I developed specifically for my students. I recorded selected books at rates that were just slightly slower than normal speech. I wanted students to be able to follow along by listening carefully to each word and phrase as it was pronounced in addition to using their fingers to point to those words and phrases as they were being read. I discovered that my own self-recorded tapes were intrinsically more valuable as instructional tools than anything I could purchase through a catalog. That was simply because students were listening to a voice they recognized—one they knew was a model of fluent reading.

Paired Readings

Paired reading is a form of choral reading done by two individuals. Typically, a pair consists of a teacher and one student—in short, an accomplished reader is paired with a struggling reader. Research on the effects of paired reading (Koskinen & Blum 1986) has shown that enormous gains in reading proficiency can be made when this strategy is used over a period of six to ten weeks. Equally important is the fact that paired readings has positive benefits for students irrespective of their grade level.

Here are a few tips that will help ensure the success of paired readings:

1. Locate a comfortable, quiet place in the classroom.

2. Make sure the two chairs are of equal size and height.

3. As appropriate, provide students with the opportunity to select the reading materials (in accordance with their instructional reading level).

4. Begin reading together. You may need to adjust your rate and intonation to those of the student. Reading at a consistent pace (perhaps a little slower than normal) is preferable to reading at a pace that is uncomfortable for the student.

5. Encourage the student to follow the text with his or her finger or some other marking tool.

6. If the student makes a mistake or stops to decode an unfamiliar word, wait for no more than three seconds and then continue reading. The emphasis should be on the smooth, fluent reading of the text. You should save any word recognition instruction for later.

7. As appropriate, encourage the student to continue reading independently. The student may wish to give you a sign (e.g., snap his or her fingers, tap his or her foot) that he or she is ready to continue reading without your "assistance."

Paired reading works best when it is done as a regularly scheduled activity. It is suggested that struggling readers participate in paired reading on a daily basis, for 10 to 20 minutes per session, for a period of not less than six weeks. This extended time frame provides readers with consistent models of reading fluency in a most supportive environment.

Student-to-Student Readings

Student-to-student readings is a modification of paired readings in which students take over the role of the teacher. For this choral reading strategy, pair an on-level reader with a below-level reader. The partners are seated side by side. The on-level reader begins by reading a selected passage to his or her partner three times. Then the partners switch roles. The reading passages used initially should be at the instructional reading level of the below-level partner (90–95 percent word recognition accuracy). As the below-level partner becomes more accomplished, the level of the passages is gradually increased.

READERS THEATRE

Briefly stated, readers theatre is fluency in action! It is reading with a purpose that is motivational and productive. Students have multiple opportunities to hear fluent reading in a variety of contexts. Students are also able to interpret and read texts with expression and comprehension.

I like to think of readers theatre as "involved reading." For students, it is an opportunity to share, a time to creatively interact with others, and a personal interpretation of what can be or could be. In fact, readers theatre holds the promise of helping children understand and appreciate the richness of language, the interpretation of that language, and how language can be a powerful vehicle for the comprehension and appreciation of different forms of literature. Readers theatre provides numerous opportunities for youngsters to make stories and literature come alive and pulsate with their own unique brand of perception and vision. In so doing, literature becomes personal and reflective—children have a breadth of opportunities to be authentic users of language. Most important, they have authentic opportunities to hear and practice fluent reading in a rich and supportive environment.

The remainder of this book demonstrates how you can use this valuable teaching tool to promote and teach fluency as a viable element of your classroom reading program and as a significant component of each student's literacy development.

CHAPTER 3

Assessing Reading Fluency

The assessment instruments on pages 27–44 are designed to help you determine the fluency levels of students in your class. They are not designed as group or class tests, but rather as individual assessment instruments that will assist you in monitoring the developing fluency levels of students.

These assessment instruments can also assist you in developing appropriate instructional groups. The success of fluency instruction lies in the fact that students within a group are relatively close in reading ability. These instruments will help ensure that process.

ADMINISTERING A FLUENCY READING PASSAGE

The assessment is to be administered one child at a time. You may wish to utilize the services of room mothers, parent volunteers, instructional aides, or other adults in administering it. Administering the assessment will take less than three minutes per child, and an entire class can be assessed in a few days (depending on your schedule of regular activities). The results from these instruments will be beneficial in deciding on the materials needed for a specific group as well as the students who can be grouped together for selected instructional activities.

NOTE: This is a simplified miscue analysis. It should be used as one element of an overall assessment process. Assessment, to be effective, must be continuous, systematic, and authentically integrated throughout the entire reading process. Assessment must also be multidisciplinary—using a variety of strategies, techniques, and procedures. The tools presented here can be effective elements in an overall reading assessment program.

To administer a fluent reading passage, follow these steps:

1. Estimate the approximate reading level of each student using the following levels as guides:

Story	Title	Grade	No. of words	Reading Level*
1A	*Sam's Hat*	Low first	220	1.0
1B	*School Is Cool!*	Mid first	208	1.5
1C	*Ducks on the Lake*	High first	217	1.9
2A	*Flowers Are Plants*	Low second	209	2.2
2B	*Cookies for Frank*	Mid second	193	2.6
2C	*Cats, Cats, Cats*	High second	208	2.9
3A	*Mr. Brown's Garden*	Low third	203	3.1
3B	*A Long Swim*	Mid third	201	3.4
3C	*Turtles All Around*	High third	200	3.9
4A	*Weird Mother*	Low fourth	219	4.1
4B	*Hummingbirds Are Fun*	Mid fourth	209	4.5
4C	*Sponges in the Ocean*	High fourth	194	4.9
5A	*Frogs are Everywhere*	Low fifth	213	5.1
5B	*Deserts: Full of Life*	Mid fifth	194	5.6
5C	*Brian's Grandfather*	High fifth	197	5.8
6A	*Gorillas Don't Play Soccer*	Low sixth	211	6.2
6B	*Lemons: Sour Fruit*	Mid sixth	196	6.6
6C	*Survival in the Wild*	High sixth	191	6.9

*Readability levels determined by the Flesch-Kincaid readability formula, which measures a) sentences per paragraph, b) words per sentence, and c) characters per word.

2. Photocopy one or more of the following reading passages—making two copies of each passage, one for you and one for the student.

3. Present the student with a reading passage and invite her or him to read it aloud to you. Time the reading with a watch or stopwatch.

4. After exactly one minute, make a mark on the exact word the student read at that point.

5. As the student reads, note each miscue the student makes by marking it on your copy of the passage. Use the marking system detailed in the handout on page 23.

HOW TO MARK AN ORAL READING PASSAGE

Example:	"Black widow spiders can be found throughout the warmer parts of the world."

Omission: Draw a line through the omitted word.

"Black widow spiders can be found throughout the ~~warmer~~ parts of the world."

Insertion: Insert a ∧ and write inserted word above text.

and

"Black widow spiders can be found throughout the warmer parts of the world."
∧

Substitution: Draw a line through the original word and write the substituted word above it.

window

"Black ~~widow~~ spiders can be found throughout the warmer parts of the world."

Reversal: Circle a reversed word and place an "R" next to it.

R

"Black widow spiders can be found throughout the warmer ⟨parts⟩ of the world."

Make note of the following, but do not count as errors:

Self-correction: Write SC next to words that the child self-corrects.

spitters (SC)

"Black widow ~~spiders~~ can be found throughout the warmer parts of the world."

Repetition: Underline portions of the text that the child repeats.

"Black widow spiders <u>can be found</u> throughout the warmer parts of the world."

Adapted from *Guided Reading in Grades 3–6: 300+ Guided Reading Strategies, Activities, and Lesson Plans for Reading Success*, by Anthony D. Fredericks (Austin, TX: Harcourt Achieve, 2001). Used by permission of the author.

EXAMPLE READING PASSAGE

Student's Name: _____ Date: _____

Story 4C: Sponges in the Ocean

~brian~

Imagine an animal with no ~brain~. Or an animal with no heart. Or ~an~ animal with

no stomach. Imagine an animal large enough to hide inside. What about an animal

                                                          all
almost 600 years old? The animals you have just imagined are real. They are all

sponges. And, <u>they are all amazing</u>! plates (sc)   ^   plates

Most people think sponges are ~plants~. Many are shaped like ~plants~. Some

sponges are fan-shaped. Others have tall, thin tubes. Some branch out. A few have big

       all
leaves. In fact, they look just like plants. But sponges are animals!

         ^
Sponges come in ~many~ colors. Some are bright orange. Others are red. Some

                                        dumb
sponges are blue or green. Many kinds have ~dull~ colors. A sponge's color comes from

tiny plants. These plants live in the skin cells]of a sponge.

Most sponges cling to rocks. They don't move around. They always stay in the

same place.

But sponges are true animals. They have babies. They catch food. They take in

oxygen. And they make waste products.

Sponges are some of the world's oldest animals. They lived during the time of

the dinosaurs. Sponges have been around for millions of years. They are amazing

creatures!

SCORING:

Omissions:	2	Self-corrections:	1
Insertions:	2	Repetitions:	1
Substitutions:	3		
Reversals:	0		

TOTAL ERRORS: 7

SCORE: 128 (total words read) - 7 (errors) = 121 (words read correctly)

Adapted from *Guided Reading in Grades 3–6: 300+ Guided Reading Strategies, Activities, and Lesson Plans for Reading Success*, by Anthony D. Fredericks (Austin, TX: Harcourt Achieve, 2001). Used by permission of the author.

From *Building Fluency with Readers Theatre: Motivational Strategies, Successful Lessons and Dynamic Scripts to Develop Fluency, Comprehension, Writing, and Vocabulary* by Anthony D. Fredericks. Westport, CT: Teacher Ideas Press. Copyright © 2008.

In the example on page 24, the student made the following miscues:

1. Substituted "brian" for "brain" (1 substitution error)
2. Omitted "an" (1 omission error)
3. Inserted "all" between "are" and "real" (1 insertion error)
4. Repeated "they are all amazing" (no error)
5. Substituted "plates" for "plants," then self-corrected (no error)
6. Substituted "plates" for "plants" (1 substitution error)
7. Inserted "all" between "they" and "look" (1 insertion error)
8. Omitted "many" (1 omission error)
9. Substituted "dumb" for "dull" (1 substitution error)

The student had seven recorded errors. The student read 128 words in a one-minute assessment. Thus, the teacher subtracts the total number of recorded errors (7) from 128. In this case, the final score is 121 WCPM (words correct per minute).

Based on the score the student obtained on the example reading passage on page 24 (121 WCPM), she or he would find reading material at the high fourth grade level (4C) to be "just right."

The teacher may wish to provide the student with one or two additional passages (at higher or lower levels) to verify the results obtained during this assessment. A variety of narrative and expository writing is suggested.

SCORING

Use the chart below to determine a student's fluency level. Target fluency levels for each elementary grade are provided as expected norms. You will note that there are norms not only for each grade level, but also for selected times of the academic year within each grade level. This supports the notion that reading fluency is dynamic and that it improves not just by grade level, but also as a direct result of the instruction we provide students throughout a single academic year.

Also indicated on the chart are fluency rates for each grade and each time of the school year, which reflect levels that would be significantly below the expected norm (S.B.E.N.). These levels (25 percent below the expected norm) would be indicative of students in need of extensive fluency instruction. They would also indicate students who may also be challenged by grade level materials in relationship to word recognition, vocabulary, and comprehension development.

Grade	Fall WCPM	SBEN	Winter WCPM	SBEN	Spring WCPM	SBEN
1	——–	——–	——–	——–	60	45
2	53	23	78	46	94	65
3	79	65	93	70	114	87
4	99	72	112	89	118	92
5	105	77	118	93	128	100
6	115	91	132	106	145	116

WCPM = words correct per minute

SBEN = significantly below expected norm (25 percent below norm)

Adapted from T. V. Rasinski, *The Fluent Reader: Oral Reading Strategies for Building Word Recognition, Fluency, and Comprehension* (New York: Scholastic, 2003)

STUDENT EXAMPLES

- Fernando has just transferred into Mr. Brooks's third-grade classroom in the middle of the year. Mr. Brooks wants to get some immediate information about Fernando and so administers a fluency reading passage (Story 3B—"A Long Swim" [mid third grade]). On the assessment, Fernando reads 95 words correct per minute. The norm for mid-third grade is 93 WCPM, so Mr. Brooks is confident that Fernando is reading at grade level for fluency.

- At the beginning of the school year, Mrs. Hause administers fluency reading passages to all her fifth-grade students. One of her students, Min Lee, obtains a score of 76 WCPM on the 5A ("Frogs Are Everywhere" [low fifth grade]) passage. Mrs. Hause checks the chart and notes than Min is reading far below grade level expectation (105 WCPM). Mrs. Hause begins planning an extensive program of fluency instruction for Min, including lots of exposure to readers theatre.

- D'Angela has always been a good reader. Notes from previous teachers have indicated her interest in books and her eagerness to spend considerable time in the school library. When Miss Markle administers a fluency reading passage (Story 4A—"Weird Mother" [low fourth grade]) to D'Angela at the start of fourth grade, she notes a score of 106 words correct per minute. Miss Markle is confident that D'Angela will do quite well in reading this year. However, when D'Angela is assessed again in January (Story 4B—"Hummingbirds Are Fun" [mid fourth grade]), she obtains a score of 109. Miss Markle is concerned that D'Angela is not making satisfactory progress in terms of her fluency development. As a result, she adjusts her instruction for D'Angela using some of the strategies outlined in chapter 2 of this book.

Please note that the fluency reading passages are only one element in a comprehensive assessment process. It is important to consider other factors that may impact a student's satisfactory progress through the reading program. Vision problems, home environment, lack of interest, and decoding deficiencies, among other things, may all influence a student's reading performance. Fluency is a single component of reading achievement, albeit a most important one, but it should be judged in the context of other reading assessments as well. On pages 27–44 are eighteen sample passages, three for each grade from 1 to 6. They are followed by two forms for assessing students' fluency levels (pp. 45–46).

Student's Name: _____ Date: _____

Story 1A: Sam's Hat

Sam had a hat. The hat was red. The hat was big. Sam had a big, red hat.

One day the wind blew. The wind blew hard. The wind blew strong. The wind blew the hat off Sam's head.

Sam said, "Oh, no!" Sam said, "Oh, boy!" Sam said, "I lost my hat!" Sam said, "I lost my big, red hat!"

Pat was Sam's friend. She saw Sam's hat in the wind. She saw Sam's hat blow away. "I will help Sam," she said.

Pat ran fast. Pat ran for the hat. Pat saw the hat. She saw the hat by the tree. Pat got the hat. She took the hat to Sam.

"You have my hat," said Sam. "Thank you," said Sam. He said, "You are a good friend. You got my hat. You got my red hat. You got my big hat. You got my big red hat."

Pat said, "I would like a hat. I would like a big hat."

So Sam and Pat went to the store. Pat saw a hat. She saw a big hat. But, it was not red. It was green. Pat got the green hat. Pat got the big hat. Pat got the big green hat.

Now, Sam has a hat. Now, Pat has a hat. Sam and Pat both have hats.

SCORING:

Omissions: _____   Self-corrections: _____

Insertions: _____   Repetitions: _____

Substitutions: _____

Reversals: _____

TOTAL ERRORS: _____

SCORE: _____ (total words read) – _____ (errors) = _____ (words read correctly)

From *Building Fluency with Readers Theatre: Motivational Strategies, Successful Lessons and Dynamic Scripts to Develop Fluency, Comprehension, Writing, and Vocabulary* by Anthony D. Fredericks. Westport, CT: Teacher Ideas Press. Copyright © 2008.

Story 1B: School Is Cool!

Welcome to our school. School is fun. School is cool! We learn new things here.

Boys go to school. Girls go to school. Teachers go to school, too. Every day busses bring many boys and girls to school. Many boys and girls go to school. A school is a great place. It's where everybody learns.

Teachers learn, too. Teachers have to go to school, too. They go to school to learn how to teach. They learn how to teach reading. They learn how to teach adding. They learn how to teach about plants. They learn lots of new things.

Boys and girls learn, too. Boys and girls learn when they go to school. They learn how to read. They learn how to add. They learn about plants. They learn lots of new things.

There is a lot to learn in school. The more we learn, the smarter we get. And, the smarter we get, the more we learn. School is a good place to learn. School is a good place to get smart. Boys and girls learn at school. Boys and girls get smart at school.

Yes, school is fun. School is cool! We learn new things when we go to school. It's a smart place to be.

SCORING:

Omissions: _____   Self-corrections: _____

Insertions: _____   Repetitions: _____

Substitutions: _____

Reversals: _____

TOTAL ERRORS: _____

SCORE: _____ (total words read) – _____ (errors) = _____ (words read correctly)

 From *Building Fluency with Readers Theatre: Motivational Strategies, Successful Lessons and Dynamic Scripts to Develop Fluency, Comprehension, Writing, and Vocabulary* by Anthony D. Fredericks. Westport, CT: Teacher Ideas Press. Copyright © 2008.

Story 1C: Ducks on the Lake

Sarah and Jerry went for a walk. They went to the park. They wanted to walk through the trees. They wanted to see the lake. They wanted to see all the ducks that came to the lake.

"Why don't we walk near the river, "said Jerry.

"That sounds like a good idea," said Sarah.

So, Jerry and Sarah walked by the river. They saw lots of birds in the sky. They saw lots of bugs on the ground. They saw lots of plants beside the river.

"This is a very pretty place," said Sarah.

"Yes, it is, said Jerry.

"I hope people take care of this place," Sarah said.

"I hope they do too," Jerry said.

When Sarah and Jerry got to the lake they saw lots of ducks. There were ducks swimming. There were ducks flying. There were ducks making lots of noise. There were ducks everywhere.

"I like it when there are lots of ducks," said Jerry

"So do I," Sarah said.

"Hey, I have some bread in my backpack. Let's give it to the ducks," said Jerry.

"That's a great idea," said Sarah.

Jerry and Sarah stood beside the lake. They threw bread to the ducks. More and more ducks came to the lake. There was lots of noise. There was lots of fun.

SCORING:

    Omissions: _____   Self-corrections: _____

    Insertions: _____   Repetitions: _____

    Substitutions: _____

    Reversals: _____

TOTAL ERRORS: _____

SCORE: _____ (total words read) – _____ (errors) = _____ (words read correctly)

Student's Name: _____ Date: _____

Story 2A: Flowers Are Plants

Plants grow. Some plants are tall. Trees are tall. Some plants grow in water. Seaweed is a water plant. Some plants grow in the ground. Roses are plants that grow in the ground. Flowers are plants, too. Let's look at a flower.

A flower has many parts. It has leaves. Leaves help the flower live. They take in sunlight. A flower needs sunlight so it can grow.

A flower has roots. Roots are at the bottom of a flower. The roots hold the flower in the ground. The roots help the flower get water. The roots help the flower get food. A flower needs roots to live.

A flower has a stem. The stem can be hard. The stem can be soft. The stem holds up the flower. And, water goes up the stem. Water goes from the roots to the flower. Water goes up the stem.

A plant has three parts. It has leaves. It has roots. And, it has a stem. A flower is a plant. It has leaves. It has roots. And, it has a stem.

Flowers are plants. A daisy is a plant. A rose is a plant. A lily is a plant. Look around. There are lots of flowers. There are lots of plants.

SCORING:

Omissions: _____   Self-corrections: _____

Insertions: _____   Repetitions: _____

Substitutions: _____

Reversals: _____

TOTAL ERRORS: _____

SCORE: _____ (total words read) – _____ (errors) = _____ (words read correctly)

From *Building Fluency with Readers Theatre: Motivational Strategies, Successful Lessons and Dynamic Scripts to Develop Fluency, Comprehension, Writing, and Vocabulary* by Anthony D. Fredericks. Westport, CT: Teacher Ideas Press. Copyright © 2008.

Story 2B: Cookies for Frank

Frank loves cookies. Frank loves the smell of cookies. Frank loves the taste of cookies. Frank loves touching cookies. Frank loves everything about cookies.

Frank would eat cookies for breakfast. Frank would eat cookies for lunch. Frank would eat cookies for dinner. Frank would eat cookies all day long.

Oh, Frank is my dog. That's right, Frank is my cookie eating dog. I don't know why he likes cookies. But, he does. He likes big cookies. He likes small cookies. He likes round cookies. He likes all kinds of cookies. He is a cookie eating dog.

When my friends visit, they bring cookies. They give the cookies to Frank. Frank eats all the cookies. He doesn't leave any crumbs. One bite, two bites, and the cookie is gone. Frank sure does like cookies.

My dad says cookies are bad for dogs. But Frank doesn't care. He likes to eat cookies all the time. He would eat cookies all day if he could. He's my cookie eating dog.

When you come to my house bring cookies. Frank will take your cookies. Frank will eat your cookies. Frank loves cookies. Frank will love you, too.

SCORING:

Omissions: _____   Self-corrections: _____

Insertions: _____   Repetitions: _____

Substitutions: _____

Reversals: _____

TOTAL ERRORS: _____

SCORE: _____ (total words read) – _____ (errors) = _____ (words read correctly)

From *Building Fluency with Readers Theatre: Motivational Strategies, Successful Lessons and Dynamic Scripts to Develop Fluency, Comprehension, Writing, and Vocabulary* by Anthony D. Fredericks. Westport, CT: Teacher Ideas Press. Copyright © 2008.

Story 2C: Cats, Cats, Cats

My grandmother has lots of cats. All the cats live in her house. She has more than ten cats. They are loud. They are noisy. They make lots of sounds when I come to visit. They are everywhere.

I like cats. But, I don't know if I like lots of cats. I don't know if I like all the cats at my grandmother's. I don't know if I like ten cats.

The cats crawl over all the chairs. The cats crawl around all the plants. The cats crawl under all the tables. Everywhere you go there are cats.

When I go to bed there is a cat on the bed. When I go to the bathroom there is a cat in the bathtub. When I go to the kitchen there is a cat on the counter. Everywhere I go there are cats.

Cats are all over the house. Cats are all around the house. They are in the garage. They are in the garden. They are in the yard. Cats are everywhere.

One day I found a cat in the car. One day I found a cat in the sink. One day I found a cat in the closet. Cats are everywhere. Everywhere you go—there's a cat!

SCORING:

Omissions: _____   Self-corrections: _____

Insertions: _____   Repetitions: _____

Substitutions: _____

Reversals: _____

TOTAL ERRORS: _____

SCORE: _____ (total words read) – _____ (errors) = _____ (words read correctly)

Student's Name: _____ Date: _____

Story 3A: Mr. Brown's Garden

Mr. Brown is my friend. He lives next door to me. Mr. Brown has a very big garden. He grows lots of vegetables in his garden. He grows beans, carrots, and corn in his garden. He also grows watermelon, pumpkins, and strawberries in his garden. His garden is very large.

Every day I go next door to help Mr. Brown. He gives me a rake to make the ground smooth. I work hard every day to help Mr. Brown. I help him keep the weeds out. I help him water his garden. It's a lot of hard work.

When we are done we sit down on the porch. We drink a glass of lemonade. We have some cookies. Sometimes, Mr. Brown tells stories. I like working hard in Mr. Brown's garden.

One day I went to help Mr. Brown. But he wasn't there. So I waited on his porch. Then, I saw something in his garden. It was a rabbit. The rabbit was eating some of the plants. I ran after the rabbit and shouted. The rabbit ran fast. I ran fast. I scared the rabbit away. Then, I went back to the porch. Guess who was waiting for me on the porch?

SCORING:

    Omissions: _____   Self-corrections: _____

    Insertions: _____   Repetitions: _____

    Substitutions: _____

    Reversals: _____

TOTAL ERRORS: _____

SCORE: _____ (total words read) – _____ (errors) = _____ (words read correctly)

Student's Name: _____ Date: _____

Story 3B: A Long Swim

The water was deep and cold. But I wasn't afraid. I jumped in and swam very hard. The rowboat seemed far away. I don't know what happened. I don't know how it got un-tied. But, I did know that I had to get it. If not, then I would be in trouble. That's because of the waterfall. The waterfall was making a very loud sound. I could hear the waterfall and it seemed close. It seemed much closer than before.

I swam very slowly. I didn't want to get tired. I had a long way to go and I didn't want to get tired. I am a good swimmer. I have been swimming all my life. I'm always careful in the water, but this was different. This time I was swimming for my life. This time I was swimming for a boat.

The boat was drifting. The boat was slowly drifting toward the waterfall. I hoped I could get it. I decided to take my time. I decided to take my time and swim very carefully. If I didn't, then there would be trouble. I'm a good swimmer, but I don't like trouble. Stroke after stroke, I swam toward the boat.

SCORING:

Omissions: _____ Self-corrections: _____

Insertions: _____ Repetitions: _____

Substitutions: _____

Reversals: _____

TOTAL ERRORS: _____

SCORE: _____ (total words read) – _____ (errors) = _____ (words read correctly)

Story 3C: Turtles All Around

Turtles are reptiles. Reptiles are the last living relatives of the dinosaurs. Other reptiles include crocodiles, snakes, and lizards.

Reptiles are cold-blooded. That means their body temperature is the same as the air or water around them. When they're cold they bask in the sun. When they're too hot, they pick a cool spot to rest.

There are about 300 kinds of turtles in the world. Some are very large. Some are very small.

Turtles can live almost anywhere in the world. But, they don't like very cold places. Some species live on land. Some live in ponds and the sea. Some live in swamps and fields. And, some live in forests or deserts.

A turtle's shell protects its whole body. The shell is made of bone. It is covered with a layer of tough scales.

A turtle's spine and ribs are attached to the upper shell. The lower shell protects its soft belly. When dangers threatens, a turtle pulls its head and legs into its shell.

Turtles do not have teeth. Most turtles have sharp beaks. They use these for eating or for defense. Turtle beaks have jagged edges that point down. This helps food go down their throat.

SCORING:

Omissions: _____   Self-corrections: _____

Insertions: _____   Repetitions: _____

Substitutions: _____

Reversals: _____

TOTAL ERRORS: _____

SCORE: _____ (total words read) – _____ (errors) = _____ (words read correctly)

Student's Name: _____ Date: _____

Story 4A: Weird Mother

Yesterday morning, my mother made me make my bed. I don't know why she always makes me do that. It just gets all messed up when I go to bed at night. She also made me put clean sheets on the bed last week. That doesn't make any sense either. After all, how can my sheets get dirty when I'm sound asleep?

Today, my mother made me clean up my room and put all my dirty clothes and stuff into the clothes hamper. I had to carry them down to the washing machine in the back of the basement. I don't know why she makes me do that. I'll just get all my shirts and pants dirty after school. Then, I'll have to take them back down to the basement again.

She also made me pick up all my toys and machines. I had to put them neatly in my closet. Why? I'll just need to take them out later.

At dinner, my mother made me eat all my vegetables. I absolutely hate, hate, hate vegetables. But she said it would make me grow healthy and strong. Of course, mothers always say that anything green is healthy for you. But, I bet they never had to eat all that healthy stuff when they were kids.

Mothers sure are peculiar!

SCORING:

Omissions: _____ Self-corrections: _____

Insertions: _____ Repetitions: _____

Substitutions: _____

Reversals: _____

TOTAL ERRORS: _____

SCORE: _____ (total words read) – _____ (errors) = _____ (words read correctly)

Story 4B: Hummingbirds Are Fun

People really love hummingbirds. It may be because of their bright colors. It may be due to their small size. Or it may be because of their playful ways. Hummingbirds are also amazing flyers.

Hummingbirds do things other birds can't. They fly backwards. They can even fly upside down. And, they can fly at great speeds.

Animals that fly need flight muscles. Flight muscles are attached to the skeleton. They provide power to the wings. Hummingbirds are almost always flying. They need very strong flight muscles to do all that flying.

Young hummingbirds learn to fly on their own. Their parents don't teach them. They begin flapping their wings in the nest. They can sometimes lift off from the nest. Their first flight is short. This flight carries them to a nearby branch. Later, they learn how to fly longer distances.

Hummingbirds can hover or stay flying over the same spot. They do this better than any other bird. Other birds have wings with many movable parts. This allows them to soar and glide.

Hummingbird wings are different. The bones in their wings don't move. At the shoulder joint the wings can move in all directions. Their wings move in a figure-8 pattern while flying. This helps them hover.

SCORING:

Omissions: _____   Self-corrections: _____

Insertions: _____   Repetitions: _____

Substitutions: _____

Reversals: _____

TOTAL ERRORS: _____

SCORE: _____ (total words read) – _____ (errors) = _____ (words read correctly)

From *Building Fluency with Readers Theatre: Motivational Strategies, Successful Lessons and Dynamic Scripts to Develop Fluency, Comprehension, Writing, and Vocabulary* by Anthony D. Fredericks. Westport, CT: Teacher Ideas Press. Copyright © 2008.

Story 4C: Sponges in the Ocean

Imagine an animal with no brain. Or an animal with no heart. Or an animal with no stomach. Imagine an animal large enough to hide inside. What about an animal almost 600 years old? The animals you have just imagined are real. They are all sponges. And, they are all amazing!

Most people think sponges are plants. Many are shaped like plants. Some sponges are fan-shaped. Others have tall thin tubes. Some branch out. A few have big leaves. In fact, they look just like plants. But, sponges are animals!

Sponges came in many colors. Some are bright orange. Others are red. Some sponges are blue or green. Many kinds have dull colors. A sponge's color comes from tiny plants. These plants live in the skin cells of a sponge.

Most sponges cling to rocks. They don't move around. They always stay in the same place.

But sponges are true animals. They have babies. They catch food. They take in oxygen. And they make waste products.

Sponges are some of the world's oldest animals. They lived during the time of the dinosaurs. Sponges have been around for millions of years. They are amazing creatures!

SCORING:

Omissions: _____   Self-corrections: _____

Insertions: _____   Repetitions: _____

Substitutions: _____

Reversals: _____

TOTAL ERRORS: _____

SCORE: _____ (total words read) – _____ (errors) = _____ (words read correctly)

From *Building Fluency with Readers Theatre: Motivational Strategies, Successful Lessons and Dynamic Scripts to Develop Fluency, Comprehension, Writing, and Vocabulary* by Anthony D. Fredericks. Westport, CT: Teacher Ideas Press. Copyright © 2008.

Student's Name: _____ Date: _____

Story 5A: Frogs Are Everywhere

Frogs are amphibians. The term amphibian is from two Greek words—*amphi* (meaning "both") and *bios* (meaning "life). Most amphibians lead a double life. They hatch from eggs in the water. And, as they grow, they move onto land.

Amphibians are also cold-blooded. Their body temperature changes with their surroundings.

There are 3,600 species of frog. Frogs live everywhere on earth. They live in tropical rainforests and desert environments. They can also be found in high mountains. The largest number of species lives in the tropics.

Frogs have compact bodies. They also have large heads. They have short front legs. These are for balance. They also have long back legs for jumping. They use their webbed feet for swimming. Most frogs average 2-5 inches in length.

Frogs have sticky tongues. They flick these out to catch their prey. But, frogs don't chew their food. Frogs swallow their meals whole.

Frogs are an important part of many food chains. They eat insects and small mammals. They also eat worms. They sometimes eat other frogs.

Frogs take in oxygen through blood vessels in the surface of their skin. They don't drink water. They absorb water through their skin. Their skin must be kept moist. This permits the transfer of oxygen and water into their bodies.

SCORING:

Omissions: _____ Self-corrections: _____

Insertions: _____ Repetitions: _____

Substitutions: _____

Reversals: _____

TOTAL ERRORS: _____

SCORE: _____ (total words read) – _____ (errors) = _____ (words read correctly)

From *Building Fluency with Readers Theatre: Motivational Strategies, Successful Lessons and Dynamic Scripts to Develop Fluency, Comprehension, Writing, and Vocabulary* by Anthony D. Fredericks. Westport, CT: Teacher Ideas Press. Copyright © 2008.

Story 5B: Deserts: Full of Life

Deserts get very little rain. Less than ten inches of rain falls a year. That means that the desert is very dry. It can also be very windy.

The desert is home to many different kinds of animals. These include mice and snakes. Spiders and turtles also live in the desert.

Some desert animals come out in the day. They are known as diurnal animals. They search for food when it's hot. Lizards are diurnal animals.

Most desert animals are nocturnal. Nocturnal animals come out at night. That's when the temperature is lower. Owls and bats are nocturnal animals.

Plants live in the desert, too. These include cacti and yuccas. The Saguaro cactus is a well-known desert plant. It can grow up to 50 feet tall. It can weigh as much as a full-grown elephant.

Cacti and other desert plants need little water. They have spines. These reduce water loss. Desert plants sometimes have long roots. These reach down deep to get water.

Most people think that deserts are dry empty places. But deserts are rich with life. Special plants and animals live there. Deserts are the perfect home for many living things.

SCORING:

Omissions: _____   Self-corrections: _____

Insertions: _____   Repetitions: _____

Substitutions: _____

Reversals: _____

TOTAL ERRORS: _____

SCORE: _____ (total words read) – _____ (errors) = _____ (words read correctly)

From *Building Fluency with Readers Theatre: Motivational Strategies, Successful Lessons and Dynamic Scripts to Develop Fluency, Comprehension, Writing, and Vocabulary* by Anthony D. Fredericks. Westport, CT: Teacher Ideas Press. Copyright © 2008.

Story 5C: Brian's Grandfather

The morning was brilliant as Brian gathered up his fishing gear and headed out the door. He had been waiting a long time for this day—ever since his grandfather had been in the accident. He wanted more than anything else to sit close to his grandfather in the canoe and cast his line out over Jackson Lake. He remembered the stories they used to tell, the tall tales they used to spin, and the laughter they used to share. Those were very special times, but things were different. Now, his grandfather was different. He just didn't know what to expect.

Brian climbed into the back of the car. His father started up the engine and pulled out of the driveway. For some reason, his father was unusually quiet this morning. He didn't say much—not even about the branches scattered across the ground after last night's thunderstorm. That's O.K., thought Brian. He didn't feel much like talking anyway. He rather save all his talking for his grandfather. The only problem was that now his grandfather couldn't talk. This was going to be a strange fishing trip, he thought. He wasn't sure he really wanted to go.

SCORING:

Omissions: _____   Self-corrections: _____

Insertions: _____   Repetitions: _____

Substitutions: _____

Reversals: _____

TOTAL ERRORS: _____

SCORE: _____ (total words read) – _____ (errors) = _____ (words read correctly)

Story 6A: Gorillas Don't Play Soccer

Last week, I went to the doctor to get a physical exam for the soccer team at school. The doctor said my height and weight were just right for my age. She was pleased with how well I have been taking care of myself. I always eat the right foods with very few snacks. I always get nine hours of sleep every night. And, I always exercise. She said I should continue practicing those habits. If so, I should be healthy my entire life.

After the exam, she said, "Just be glad you're not a gorilla. You weigh 70 pounds, but a ten-year-old female gorilla weights 200 pounds and her ten-year-old brother might weigh 450 pounds. Can you imagine a 450 pound soccer player?" she asked.

I told her that a gorilla might be a very interesting player to have on a soccer team. But I wouldn't want to play a game against that team. It could be pretty ugly!

I live in Oregon, but I know a lot about gorillas. That's because I have an aunt who is a wildlife photographer. She has traveled to many countries around the world taking photographs for various magazines. She likes to takes photos high in the mountains of Africa. That's where gorillas live.

SCORING:

Omissions: _____   Self-corrections: _____

Insertions: _____   Repetitions: _____

Substitutions: _____

Reversals: _____

TOTAL ERRORS: _____

SCORE: _____ (total words read) – _____ (errors) = _____ (words read correctly)

Story 6B: Lemons: Sour Fruit

What do you think when you hear the word "lemons?" Do you think about lemonade? What about lemon meringue pie? Or lemon custard? Like many people, you probably think about food items. But lemons are also used in household products. Some of them are in your home right now. These include furniture polishes and perfumes. Cosmetics and dish washing soap also have lemon juice.

Lemons are used to fight diseases. Scurvy is a deadly disease. It's caused by a lack of vitamin C. English sailors used to carry lemons on their ships. The lemon juice saved them from getting scurvy.

Lemons came from India. Now, they are found throughout the world. Lemons are grown in sub-tropical regions. In this country, most lemons are grown in southern California. Some are grown in Texas. Lemon orchards are also found in central Florida. But, California is the lemon-growing center of the U.S.

Lemon trees are evergreens. They stay green all year long. Some lemon trees grow up to twenty feet tall. They prefer warm temperatures. They grow best in direct sunlight. They also like acidic soil. Lemons are a citrus fruit. Limes, oranges, and grapefruits are also citrus fruits.

SCORING:

Omissions: _____   Self-corrections: _____

Insertions: _____   Repetitions: _____

Substitutions: _____

Reversals: _____

TOTAL ERRORS: _____

SCORE: _____ (total words read) – _____ (errors) = _____ (words read correctly)

Student's Name:_____ Date:_____

Story 6C: Survival in the Wild

If somebody at school stepped on your foot, what would you do? Would you get angry? Would you step on that person's foot? Would you walk away? Would you talk with that person? Your foot might hurt for a while and you may be upset. But, I don't think you would inject a deadly poison into that person.

Your community or school is relatively safe. Yet, life in the wild is full of dangers. In fact, most animals spend their lives trying to get enough food to eat while avoiding becoming a food source for other creatures. This is known as "survival of the fittest." That means that animals who are able to find enough food and protect themselves from other animals can live long enough to produce another generation. This ensures the continuation of their species.

In order to survive, many animals have defense mechanisms. That is, they have abilities or features which they use for protection from predators (animals that hunt them). Some animals, such as chameleons, can camouflage themselves. Their enemies cannot locate them in the thick underbrush. Other animals have claws or poison glands to protect themselves.

SCORING:

Omissions: _____   Self-corrections: _____

Insertions: _____   Repetitions: _____

Substitutions: _____

Reversals: _____

TOTAL ERRORS: _____

SCORE: _____ (total words read) – _____ (errors) = _____ (words read correctly)

Fluency Reading Passage Scoring Rubric

DIRECTIONS: Administer an assessment story to a student. After scoring the reading, look at the chart below. Fill in the target fluency levels for your grade using the scoring chart (with norms) on page 25. Then record the assessed WCPM score the student achieves on the selected test. Then place a check mark in one of the three following columns to indicate if the student is A) significantly above his/her expected fluency level, B) on target for his/her fluency level, or C) significantly below (25 percent or more) his/her expected fluency level. You may wish to give the student a story that is one level above and another that is one level below the first story. That will help you pinpoint a more accurate fluency level for the student.

Name: _____

Grade: _____

	Target Norm (WCPM)	Assessed Norm (WCPM.)	High	On Target	Low
Fall Date:					
Winter Date:					
Spring Date:					

Fluency Assessment Grid

DIRECTIONS: Write the names of all your students down the left side of this grid. After each student's name, record the level (1A, 3B, 6C) of the story used to assess his/her fluency performance. Then place a check mark (on target) or an "X" (below expectation) in the column that indicates when the assessment was administered. After completing this chart you will be able to note the students who are making satisfactory progress in their fluency development through the year as well as those students who are not progressing in an appropriate manner. This will give you the opportunity to provide individual students or groups of students will appropriate fluency activities such as readers theatre and other strategies, as enumerated in chapter 2 of this book.

Name	Story Level	Fall	Winter	Spring

✓ = On Target

X = Below Expectation

COMPREHENSION CHECKS

The oral reading passages presented in the previous section are primarily designed to assist you in identifying students' fluency levels; they are but one element in an overall assessment program. Undoubtedly you may discover students who read a passage at an appropriate level of fluency, but will be unable to comprehend what they read. In essence, a simple fluency check does not (and is not intended to) reflect the comprehension of a passage.

As part of an overall reading assessment, you may wish to gauge individual student levels of comprehension. Following are comprehension questions for each of the stories presented in the previous section. These questions are based on Bloom's taxonomy (Bloom et al. 1956) and contain six levels arranged in hierarchical form, from the least complex to the most complex:

1. **Knowledge.** Questions at this level are used to determine whether students can recall or identify factual information in text.

2. **Comprehension.** These questions are those in which students must organize, assemble, or combine factual information into a grouping or cluster of ideas.

3. **Application.** At the application level, students are asked to take information they already know and apply it to a new situation.

4. **Analysis.** At the analysis level students must be able to identify the elements making up the whole, see the relationships of the parts, and break down the whole into its related parts.

5. **Synthesis.** Synthesis is the ability to combine two or more facts into a new whole—it is the level that elicits and rewards creativity.

6. **Evaluation.** Evaluation requires an individual to make a judgment about something—that is, to make a personal statement about the value, worth, or rank of specific information.

Directions: After a student has completed the oral reading of a passage, you may wish to ask her or him the applicable questions from the outline below. Ask all six questions for each passage. Note the student's responses and compare the number of correct responses to this chart.

❖ **Independent Level:** The student can read the text independently with 95 percent or better comprehension. *Number of correct questions: 6.*

❖ **Instructional Level:** The student can read the text with some instructional assistance and with 90–95 percent comprehension. *Number of correct questions: 5.*

❖ **Frustration Level:** The student is frustrated by the text and has a comprehension level of 75 percent or below. *Number of correct questions: 0–4.*

Please keep in mind that this part of the assessment process is optional and does not have to be part of a reading program focused on fluency development. However, this "quick and easy" comprehension assessment can yield some important data in combination with oral reading abilities.

Story 1A

1. What blew off Sam's head? (*a hat*)
2. What were the colors of the two hats? (*red, green*)
3. Why did Sam's hat blow away? (*the wind*)
4. What was the difference between Sam's hat and Pat's hat? (*one red, one green*)
5. What would you need to do to keep a hat on your head? (*tie it down*)
6. If you had a hat, what color would it be?

Story 1B

1. Where did this story take place? (*at school*)
2. Who goes to school? (*boys, girls, teachers*)
3. Why do people go to school? (*to learn new things*)
4. Why is school important? (*a place to learn*)
5. What are some other places where you can learn? (*home, museum, library*)
6. What do you like most about school?

Story 1C

1. Where did Sarah and Jerry go? (*to the park*)
2. What were some of the things they saw? (*birds, bugs, plants, ducks*)
3. Where else would you see ducks? (*river, stream, other water sources*)
4. What is something all ducks do? (*eat, swim*)
5. Besides bread, what else do ducks eat? (*plants, small animals*)
6. What do you like most about ducks?

Story 2A

1. Where do plants grow? (*in the ground*)
2. What are three things a flower has? (*roots, stem, leaves*)
3. Why do flowers have stems? (*to hold them up, to transport water*)
4. What are some examples of flowers? (*daisy, rose, lily*)
5. Where are some places you might see flowers? (*garden, along road, back yard*)
6. What is your favorite flower?

Story 2B

1. What does Frank like to eat? (*cookies*)
2. When does Frank eat cookies? (*breakfast, lunch, dinner*)
3. Why does Frank enjoy cookies? (*sweet, tasty, chewy, crunchy*)
4. What kinds of cookies does Frank like to eat? (*big, small, round, all kinds*)
5. What other things do you think Frank would eat? (*candy, sweet items*)
6. Would you like to have a dog like Frank?

Story 2C

1. Who has lots of cats? (*grandmother*)
2. Where are all the cats in the house? (*on chairs, under tables, on the bed, in the bathroom*)
3. Why does the grandmother have so many cats? (*she likes them*)
4. What would the narrator find if he/she looked in the bedroom? (*cats*)
5. Where are some places outside where cats would be? (*in a garden, in a tree, yard*)
6. What do you enjoy most about cats?

Story 3A

1. What does Mr. Brown have? (*a big garden*)
2. What does Mr. Brown grow? (*beans, carrots, corn, watermelons, pumpkins, strawberries*)
3. Why does Mr. Brown grow vegetables in his garden? (*to eat*)
4. Why do you think Mr. Brown and the narrator are friends? (*they work together*)
5. What are some other places where you would find vegetables (*farm, store*)
6. What is your favorite vegetable?

Story 3B

1. What was the narrator swimming toward? (*the boat*)
2. Describe how the swimmer was swimming. (*deliberate strokes, carefully, slow*)
3. What would happen if the swimmer swam fast? (*might get tired*)
4. Why was the waterfall important? (*it might be dangerous*)
5. How else could the narrator have retrieved the boat? (*helicopter, long rope*)
6. Do you think the narrator did the right thing?

Story 3C

1. Name some reptiles. (*turtles, crocodiles, alligators, snakes, lizards*)
2. What are some reptile characteristics? (*cold-blooded, related to dinosaurs*)
3. Why do turtles have shells? (*protection*)
4. Why don't turtles live in arctic regions? (*too cold, can't survive*)
5. What would you need to include in a turtle terrarium? (*heat, food, shade*)
6. What is the most amazing fact about turtles?

Story 4A

1. Where did the narrator put the clothes? (*in the hamper*)
2. What kinds of things did the narrator have to pick up? (*clothes, toys*)
3. What would happen if the clothes were left on the floor? (*mother would get angry*)
4. Where would the toys be placed? (*in a toy box*)
5. Why do the clothes have to be picked up? (*to be washed, for neatness*)
6. How is the narrator like you?

Story 4B

1.   Animals that fly need what? (*flight muscles*)

2.   What are some things hummingbirds do that other birds can't? (*fly backward, fly upside down, fly fast*)

3.   Why do hummingbirds need such strong muscles? (*they fly almost all the time*)

4.   Why is a hummingbird's first flight so short? (*wings not developed, too young*)

5.   How are hummingbird wings different from other birds' wings? (*bones in wings don't move*)

6.   What do you enjoy most about hummingbirds?

Story 4C

1.   What is an animal with no heart? (*sponge*)

2.   What do all animals do? (*have babies, catch food, take in oxygen, make waste products*)

3.   Why don't sponges move? (*no form of locomotion, easier to catch food*)

4.   What are some similarities between sponges and plants? (*have roots, stay in same place, some have branches*)

5.   If you had a pet sponge, what would it need? (*water, food*)

6.   What was the most amazing fact about sponges?

Story 5A

1.   Are frogs warm-blooded or cold-blooded? (*cold-blooded*)

2.   What does the word "amphibian" mean? (*double life, lives on land & in water*)

3.   Why do frogs have sticky tongues? (*to catch their prey*)

4.   How are frogs able to jump so well? (*stout bodies, long back legs*)

5.   What are some places you might find frogs? (*ponds, lakes, rivers, streams*)

6.   What else would you like to learn about frogs?

Story 5B

1.   How much rain does a desert get? (*less than 10 inches*)

2.   What kinds of animals live in a desert? (*mice, snakes, spiders, turtles*)

3.   Why are most desert animals nocturnal? (*cooler in the night, easier to hunt prey*)

4.   How do cactus plants prevent water loss? (*spines, waxy covering, long roots*)

5.   What are some places where you might find deserts in the United States? (*Arizona, Colorado, Utah, New Mexico, California, Nevada*)

6.   What do you think would be challenging about living in the desert?

Story 5C

1.   What time of day did this story take place? (*in the morning*)

2.   What were Brian and his grandfather going to do? (*go fishing*)

3.   Why did Brian want to "cast his line?" (*keep it away from the boat, catch fish*)

4.   How did the accident change the grandfather? (*injured him, made him sad*)

5. Why did Brian want to sit close to his grandfather? (*to get to know him better, to share stories, to share laughter*)

6. What do you think Brian will discover about his grandfather?

Story 6A

1. What did the narrator do at the doctor's? (*get a physical exam*)

2. How does the narrator take care of herself? (*eats right, sleeps, exercises*)

3. Why didn't the narrator want to play soccer with a gorilla? (*too big, ugly*)

4. What are some of the major differences between gorillas and people? (*lots of hair, heavy weight*)

5. Where do most gorillas live? (*Africa*)

6. Would you like to play soccer with a gorilla?

Story 6B

1. What disease is prevented by eating lemons? (*scurvy*)

2. What are some food products made from lemons? (*lemonade, lemon custard, lemon meringue pie*)

3. Why are lemons so popular? (*lots of products, lots of uses*)

4. What type of climate or environment would be best to grow lemons? (*semitropical*)

5. How long have lemons been around? (*hundreds of years*)

6. What is your favorite product made from lemons?

Story 6C

1. What is an animal that can camouflage itself? (*chameleons*)

2. What do most animals spend their lives doing? (*avoiding becoming prey while getting enough food to eat*)

3. Why do animals have defense mechanisms? (*to protect themselves*)

4. What are some of the ways in which animals protect themselves? (*claws, poison glands*)

5. Why do some animals have colors that are similar to the plants on which they live? (*for camouflage*)

6. What did you enjoy most about this story?

CHAPTER 4

What Is Readers Theatre?

Say the words "Once upon a time . . ." to any adult, and you will probably see a smile slip across his or her face. Those are magical words—words that conjure up legends, fairy tales, and stories of long ago. For most of us, they bring back pleasant memories of someone (our parents or a favorite teacher) reading (aloud) a story or book. Those words may remind us of simpler times—times long before we had to worry about home mortgages, saving for our kids' college tuition, retirement plans, or even behavioral objectives. The memories were sweet and the recollections were always pleasurable.

Think how those same four words might affect the students with whom you work. Think of the mental journeys or creative adventures you can share with youngsters as you lead them through the magical world of children's literature. Imaginations are stimulated and minds are filled with the delicious sounds of language in action! It is that language—the language of feeling, emotion, and passion—that excites youngsters and helps them appreciate the role literature plays in their everyday lives (as it has for generations).

And what better way to bring children's literature alive than through the magic of readers theatre? Readers theatre offers youngsters interesting and unique insights into the utility of language and its value in both its printed and oral forms. It is "language arts" in its purest form: it boosts listening and speaking skills, enhances writing abilities, powers reading development, develops positive self-concepts, and transforms reluctant readers into energized readers. Quite simply, it is literature brought to life and life brought to literature.

WHAT IS READERS THEATRE?

The magic of storytelling has been a tradition of every culture and civilization since the dawn of language. It binds human beings and celebrates their heritage as no other language art can. It is part and parcel of the human experience, because it underscores the values and experiences we cherish as well as those we seek to share with each other. Nowhere is this more important than in today's classroom or library. Perhaps it is a natural part of who we are that stories command our attention and help us appreciate the values, ideas, and traditions we hold dear. So, too, should students have those same experiences and pleasures.

Storytelling conjures up all sorts of visions and possibilities: faraway lands, magnificent adventures, enchanted princes, beautiful princesses, evil wizards and wicked witches, a few dragons and demons, a couple of castles and cottages, perhaps a mysterious forest or two, and certainly tales of mystery, intrigue, and adventure. These are stories of tradition and timelessness, tales that enchant, mystify, and excite through a marvelous weaving of characters, settings, and plots that have stood the test of time. Our senses are stimulated, our mental images are energized, and our experiences are fortified through the magic of storytelling.

Storytelling is also a way of sharing the power and intrigue of language. I suppose part of my belief that storytelling is the quintessential classroom activity lies in the fact that it is an opportunity to bring life, vitality, and substance to the two-dimensional letters and words on a printed page. It is also an interpersonal activity, a "never-fail" way to connect with minds and souls and hearts.

When children are provided with regular opportunities to become storytellers, they develop a personal stake in the literature shared. They also begin to cultivate personal interpretations of that literature, which leads to higher levels of appreciation and comprehension. Practicing and performing stories is an involvement endeavor, one that demonstrates and utilizes numerous languaging activities.

Readers theatre is a storytelling device that stimulates the imagination and promotes *all* of the language arts. Simply stated, it is an oral interpretation of a piece of literature read in a dramatic style. Teachers all across the country have long promoted the powerful benefits of drama for their students: positive emotional growth, increased levels of motivation, and absolute engagement in the tasks of learning.

Readers theatre is an act of involvement, an opportunity to share, a time to creatively interact with others, and a personal interpretation of what can or could be. It provides numerous opportunities for youngsters to make stories and literature come alive and pulsate with their own unique brand of perception and vision. In so doing, literature becomes personal and reflective; children have a breadth of opportunities to be authentic users of language. As Sam Sebesta, a well-known teacher educator, states:

> Readers Theatre introduces the element of drama into literacy learning and magically transforms the classroom into a stage. During Readers Theatre time, the reader is at center stage, totally absorbed in reading. The reader is a star. (Sebesta 2003)

WHAT YOUR PRINCIPAL NEEDS TO KNOW

In this era of accountability and standards-based education, many educators want to know if classroom practices—whether traditional or innovative—have an impact on the literacy growth of students. Significant research on the use of readers theatre in elementary classrooms has demonstrated its positive effects on comprehension development, motivation to read, attitudes toward learning, and appreciation of reading as a lifelong skill.

What follows is a brief summary of some significant research on the impact of readers theatre on the literacy growth of students. Feel free to share this information with interested (or questioning) administrators, parents, or community members. Suffice it to say, readers theatre is a "research-based practice" that has been demonstrated to have a significant and powerful impact on students' reading growth and development.

❖ "Creative and critical thinking are enhanced through the utilization of readers theatre. Children are active participants in the interpretation and delivery of a story; as such, they develop thinking skills that are divergent rather than convergent, and interpretive skills that are supported rather than directed." (Fredericks 2007)

❖ "Readers theatre provides an active, analytical framework for reading and helps students to understand and interpret what they read." (Wolf 1998)

❖ "Readers theatre provides troubled readers with successful reading experiences; it can reshape images of failure into those of success and accomplishment. Readers theatre forms a bridge between troubled reading to supported reading, and ultimately, independent reading." (Dixon et al. 1996)

❖ "Readers theatre [promotes] oral reading fluency, as children [explore] and [interpret] the meaning of literature." (Martinez et al. 1999)

❖ "We are gaining evidence from classroom research that readers theatre yields improvements in students' word recognition, fluency, and comprehension." (Rasinski 2003)

❖ "[Readers theatre] is valuable for non-English speaking children or non-fluent readers. Readers theatre provides them with positive models of language usage and interpretation. . . . It allows them to see 'language in action' and the various ways in which language can be used." (Fredericks 2001)

❖ "Even resistant readers eagerly engage in practicing for readers theatre performance, reading and rereading scripts many times." (Tyler & Chard, 2000)

❖ "Second graders who did readers theatre on a regular basis made, on average, more than a year's growth in reading." (Strecker et al. 1999)

❖ "As students take on the roles of characters (in readers theatre, for example), they also take on the roles of competent readers." (Fredericks 2008a, 2008b)

The research is clear: Classroom teachers and librarians who make readers theatre a regular and systematic component of their literacy instruction and introduction to literature will be providing those students with positive opportunities to succeed in all aspects of reading growth and development. Word recognition, vocabulary, fluency, and comprehension can all be enhanced considerably when readers theatre becomes part of the educational offerings in any classroom or library.

WHAT IS THE VALUE OF READERS THEATRE?

Above and beyond the substantive research supporting the use of readers theatre as a positive classroom and library activity, here's what I like so much about readers theatre: It allows children to breathe life and substance into literature, an interpretation that is neither right nor wrong, since it will be colored by kids' unique perspectives, experiences, and vision. The reader's interpretation of a piece of literature is intrinsically more valuable than some predetermined "translation" that might be found in a teacher's manual, for example.

Many teachers subscribe to the notion that reading involves an active and energetic relationship between the reader and the text. That is, the reader–text relationship is reciprocal and involves the characteristics of the reader as well as the nature of the material (Fredericks 2001). This philosophy of reading has particular applications for teachers and librarians building effective literacy programs. It also serves as a foundation for the implementation and effectiveness of readers theatre.

With that in mind, here are some of the many educational values I see in readers theatre. These have come from my own work with youngsters as a former classroom teacher and reading specialist, a thorough review of the literature on readers theatre, as well as my observations of, and conversations with, classroom teachers throughout the United States and Canada.

1. Readers theatre brings literature to life! For many students, particularly those struggling with reading, words on a page often appear as "lifeless characters"—devoid of expression, emotion, or involvement. Readers theatre, however, provides both accomplished and struggling readers with a lively and active interpretation of books. Readers get to see and participate in a personal interpretation and involvement process that "activates" the words, characters, and plots of stories.

2. Students are connected to real literature in authentic situations. They are exposed to quality literature from a wide range of authors and a wide range of genres. Many readers theatre scripts are based on real literature sources, and students can begin developing their own interpretations of literature through the creation of their own scripts based on those books. In fact, one of the best ways to help children enjoy and extend their appreciation of good books is by encouraging them to write and perform readers theatre productions after reading an appropriate piece of literature. Readers theatre can also be used to introduce children to good literature. After performing a readers theatre script, children will be stimulated to read the original source, not to compare, but rather to extend their learning opportunities. Readers theatre may precede the reading of a related book or be used as an appropriate follow-up to the reading (oral or silent) of a good book. Quality literature and readers theatre are mutually complementary elements of the overall literacy program that underscore children's active engagement in text.

3. Children can learn about the major features of children's literature: plot, theme, setting, point of view, and characterization. This occurs when they are provided with opportunities to design and construct their own readers theatre scripts (after experiencing prepared scripts such as those in this book or scripts that you create using books and literature shared in regular reading instruction).

4. Readers theatre helps students focus on the integration of all the language arts: reading, writing, speaking, and listening. Children begin to see that effective communication and the comprehension of text are inexorably intertwined. Most state standards in the language arts, and all research reports about best practices in literacy, underscore literacy as an integrated series of related components. In other words, literacy growth is not just growth in reading—it is the development of reading in concert with the other language arts. The next section ("Hey, What about Standards?") provides the specific connections between each of the English/Language Arts Standards and readers theatre. It's interesting to note how readers theatre promotes, enhances, and solidifies students' mastery of 11 of the 12 English/Language Arts Standards (92 percent).

5. Teachers and librarians have also discovered that readers theatre is an excellent way to enhance the development of important communication skills. Voice projection, intonation, inflection, and pronunciation skills are all promoted throughout any readers theatre production. This places more value on the processes of literacy instruction than on the products (e.g., standardized test scores).

6. Readers theatre allows children to experience stories in a supportive and nonthreatening format that underscores their active involvement. This is particularly beneficial for those students who are struggling with reading. Struggling readers often envision reading as something "done *to* a text" rather than as something "done *with* a text." This shift

in perspective is often a critical factor in the success youngsters can eventually enjoy in reading. A change in attitude, a change in viewpoints, and a change in purpose often lead below-level readers to some new and interesting discoveries. Motivation, confidence, and outlook are all positively affected when students become the players and the performers. Equally important, the development and enhancement of self-concept is facilitated through readers theatre. Because children are working in concert with other children in a supportive atmosphere, their self-esteem mushrooms accordingly.

7. Readers theatre stimulates the imagination and the creation of visual images. A process of mental imagery helps readers construct "mind pictures" that serve as a way to tie together predictions, background knowledge, and textual knowledge in a satisfying experience. Once images are created, they become a permanent part of long-term memory. Just as important, they assist in the development of independent readers who are "connected" with the stories they read. It has been substantiated that when youngsters are provided with opportunities to create their own mental images, their comprehension and appreciation of a piece of writing will be enhanced considerably.

8. The central goal of reading instruction is comprehension. Comprehension is based on one's ability to make sense of printed materials. It goes beyond one's ability to remember details or recall factual information from text. Several researchers (Wiggens & McTighe 1998; Wiske 1998) suggest that students comprehend when they are able to a) connect new knowledge to their prior knowledge, b) interpret what they learn, c) apply their knowledge to new situations, and d) explain and predict events and actions. Readers theatre provides students with rich opportunities to accomplish all four elements of reading comprehension in a learning environment that is both supportive and engaged. Giving meaning to print is one of the major results of readers theatre, just as it is one of the major results of comprehension instruction.

9. Cunningham and Allington (2003) have shown that readers theatre is a perfect multilevel activity that allows teachers to group students heterogeneously rather than by ability, as is done in traditional reading programs. It provides teachers with varied options to group students by interest and desire rather than by reading level. Parts can be assigned that are sufficiently challenging (instructional level) without forcing students to deal with material at their frustration level of reading. Because students will have multiple opportunities to practice their "reading materials" at an appropriate level, they will be able to achieve levels of both competence and fluency not normally provided in more traditional "round robin" reading activities.

10. Readers theatre is a participatory event. The characters as well as the audience are all intimately involved in the design, structure, and delivery of the story. Children begin to realize that reading is not a solitary activity, but rather one that can be shared and discussed with others. As a result, readers theatre enhances the development of cooperative learning strategies. Not only does readers theatre require youngsters to work together toward a common goal, but even more important, it supports their efforts in doing so.

11. Because it is the performance that drives readers theatre, children are given more opportunities to invest themselves and their personalities in the production of a readers theatre. The same story may be subject to several different presentations depending on the group or the individual youngsters involved.

12. When children are provided with opportunities to write or script their own readers theatre, their writing abilities are supported and encouraged. As children become familiar with the design and format of readers theatre scripts, they can begin to utilize their creative talents in designing their own scripts. Readers theatre also exposes students to many examples of quality literature. That literature serves as positive models for their own writing. Just as authors of children's books write for authentic purposes (e.g., to entertain, to inform, to convince), so too

will students understand the value of purposeful writing as they craft original readers theatre scripts or adaptations from popular books and stories.

13. Readers theatre is fun! Children of all ages have delighted in using readers theatre for many years. It is delightful and stimulating, encouraging and fascinating, relevant and personal. It is a classroom or library activity filled with a cornucopia of instructional possibilities and educational ventures.

"HEY, WHAT ABOUT STANDARDS?"

In response to a demand for a cohesive set of standards that address overall curriculum design and comprehensive student performance expectations in reading and language arts education, the International Reading Association, in concert with the National Council of Teachers of English, developed and promulgated the *IRA/NCTE Standards for the English Language Arts.* These standards provide a focused outline of the essential components of a well-structured language arts curriculum.

The 12 standards place an emphasis on literacy development as a lifelong process—one that starts well before youngsters enter school and continues throughout their lives. Thus, these standards are intentionally integrative and multidisciplinary. Just as important, they support and underscore the values of readers theatre (see above) as a multipurpose language arts activity—one appropriate for both classroom and library.

The following chart provides an abridged version of the *Standards for the English Language Arts.* Along with each standard (as appropriate) is how readers theatre serves as a valuable and innovative teaching tool in support of those standards.

English/Language Arts Standards*	Readers Theatre Support
1. Students are engaged in a wide variety of print and nonprint resources.	Readers theatre introduces students to a wealth of literature from a variety of literary sources.
2. Students are exposed to many genres of literature.	Readers theatre offers students a range of reading materials that span the eight basic genres of children's literature.
3. Students use many reading strategies to comprehend text.	Readers theatre invites students to assume an active role in comprehension development through their engagement and participation.
4. Students communicate in a variety of ways.	Readers theatre invites students to practice reading, writing, listening, and speaking in an enjoyable and educative process.
5. Students learn through writing.	Readers theatre encourages students to develop their own scripts and share them with a receptive audience.
6. Students use a variety of language conventions to understand text.	Readers theatre encourages students to discuss and understand how language conveys ideas.

7.	Students are involved in personally meaningful research projects.	Readers theatre invites youngsters to examine and explore stories from a wide range of perspectives.
8.	Students are comfortable with technology.	
9.	Students gain an appreciation of language in a variety of venues.	Readers theatre encourages students to look at language and language use in a host of educational formats.
10.	Non-English-speaking students develop competencies in all the language arts.	Readers theatre offers models of English use in a fun and engaging format.
11.	Students are members of a host of literacy communities.	Readers theatre provides creative, investigative, and dynamic opportunities to see language in action.
12.	Students use language for personal reasons.	Readers theatre offers innumerable opportunities for students to engage in personally enriching language activities.

*Modified and abridged from *Standards for the English Language Arts*, International Reading Association/National Council of Teachers of English, 1996

When reviewing these standards, it should become evident that many standards can be promoted through the regular and systematic introduction of readers theatre into the elementary language arts curriculum. Equally important is that those standards assist teachers and librarians in validating the impact and significance of readers theatre as a viable and valuable instructional tool—in language arts and throughout the entire elementary curriculum.

CHAPTER 5

Readers Theatre Develops Fluency

Amy Wingate has been teaching fourth grade in Albuquerque, New Mexico, for five years. She has a "delicious range of reading abilities" in her class, with students reading anywhere from the first- to the sixth-grade level. With such a diversity, it has always been a challenge for Amy to select and use appropriate reading materials. In light of national and state standards, she is also challenged to help her students achieve appropriate levels of reading growth over the course of the academic year.

In an interview, Amy was adamant about helping her students achieve a "smoothness of reading—a deliberate and conscious awareness and practice of what good readers do when they read for pleasure." She was aware of the role of fluency as a significant area of emphasis throughout the reading program—an area that assisted students in achieving the "smoothness" she was searching for.

For Amy, reading was like a robust and emotional song—full of ardor and exciting ventures in every stanza and every note. Amy began each school day reading a piece of children's literature or several chapters from a favorite book. Her reading was filled with passion, emotion, and energy. She quickly "got into" each and every story she read aloud to her students. She became absorbed by a story—her reading overflowed with high energy, intrigue, and enthusiasm. Students were literally "on the edge of their seats" as they enjoyed the wonderful emphasis Amy put into each word, phrase and sentence. After 15 minutes—and when the schedule dictated that she address the necessary language arts curriculum—Amy's students would beg, plead, and demand that she continue reading, whether it was another chapter, another book, or just another paragraph. Each day her students witnessed a master of oral reading, and they were spellbound by her ability to bring life and enthusiasm to each and every word she shared with them.

Amy wanted her students to experience the same thrill and enjoyment she got from reading in their own reading journeys. After attending a workshop presented by the author of this book, she decided that readers theatre would be the ideal way to help her students feel that energy AND provide them with realistic opportunities to enhance their fluency development. In the workshop, Amy learned that readers theatre has the capacity to engage students in authentic reading experiences that influence fluency development and comprehension achievement. With the diversity of readers in her classroom, Amy felt that readers theatre would be "just the ticket" for helping her students become part of the same passionate reading process that she enjoyed.

FLUENCY AND READERS THEATRE

Reading researchers have identified five primary areas of reading instruction for all readers:

- phonemic awareness

- phonics

- fluency

- vocabulary

- comprehension

Fluency is the ability to read text accurately and quickly. It is reading in which words are recognized automatically. When fluent readers read, they group words quickly to help them gain meaning from what they read. Their oral reading sounds natural and their silent reading is smooth and unencumbered by an overemphasis on word-by-word analysis. Fluent readers do not need to concentrate on the decoding of words; rather, they can direct their attention to their comprehension of text. In short, fluent readers are able to recognize words and comprehend at the same time. They are able to make connections between their background knowledge and ideas in a book or other piece of writing. I often like to think of fluency as the essential stepping stone between phonetic ability and comprehension.

It's important to remember that fluency is something that develops over time. Fluency instruction must be integrated into all aspects of the reading program as the "bridge" that students need to be successful "comprehenders." Fluency is not an isolated element of the reading curriculum—rather, it is an essential component that models and provides active involvement opportunities for students as they transition from decoding to comprehension. A study by the National Assessment of Educational Progress (National Assessment Governing Board 2002) found a direct correlation between fluency and reading comprehension. In fact, students who score low on measures of fluency also score low on measures of comprehension. The implication was that efforts designed to foster fluency development will have a direct impact on students' growth and development in comprehension development.

It is not surprising that one of the most effective ways teachers and librarians can promote fluency development is through the use of readers theatre. Its advantages are twofold:

- It offers positive models of fluent reading, as demonstrated by a teacher or other accomplished readers.

- It provides readers with a legitimate reason for re-reading text in an enjoyable and engaging format.

Students should practice fluency in authentic texts and in authentic situations. Reading will be portrayed as a pleasurable activity—it has both purpose and interest. As students take on the roles of characters (in readers theatre, for example), they also take on the roles of competent readers.

Readers theatre is an instructional method that enhances reading fluency. In one research study (Martinez et al. 1999), readers theatre was integrated into two second-grade classrooms over a 10-week period. Each of the teachers provided students with 30 minutes of readers theatre instruction per day. Time was available for students to practice their scripts in the classroom, and they were also encouraged to take their scripts home for additional practice.

Each Friday, readers theatre presentations were scheduled in the two classrooms. Classmates, other students, parents, and the school principal were all part of the audience. The live audience provided students with an opportunity to share their reading with an appreciative and receptive group.

Reading performance of all the students in the two classrooms was assessed both prior to the initiation of the readers theatre program as well as at its conclusion. Here are some of the results reported:

1. Students in the two readers theatre classrooms demonstrated a fluency gain of 17 words per minute in reading unrehearsed text. Students in other classrooms (where readers theatre was not used) made gains of fewer than 7 words per minute in their fluency rates.

2. Students in the two readers theatre classrooms made an overall gain of 1.1 years in reading comprehension growth (again, this project only lasted for 10 weeks). The average gain in the other classrooms (where readers theatre was not used) was less than half of what was discovered in the project classrooms.

The authors of this study concluded that readers theatre "promoted oral reading fluency, as children explored and interpreted the meaning of literature." Suffice it to say that the implementation of readers theatre in a classroom reading program for an entire year can promote undeniable and significant gains in reading ability in excess of what might normally be expected. In fact, when teachers and librarians incorporate readers theatre into their respective programs, youngsters are offered multiple opportunities to understand the natural rhythm and flow of language in an environment that promotes fluency and enhances comprehension. What more could any teacher ask for?

BEYOND REPEATED READINGS

You'll recall from your reading of chapter 2 that the strategy of repeated readings is one of the most effective ways to help students become fluent readers. Backed by decades of research, repeated readings is a tested and proven method for increasing reading fluency in all elementary classrooms (National Reading Panel 2000). Its major "downside," however, is that students are subjected to reading a selection of text over and over again. As you might imagine, their interest wanes, their motivation lags, and their attention suffers. (Just imagine having to read the same newspaper article 10, 20, or 30 times, until you can pronounce every word precisely and efficiently.)

On the other hand, readers theatre embraces all the benefits of repeated readings, with none of its shortcomings. I like to think of readers theatre as "repeated reading for *authentic* reasons." Readers theater gives repeated readings a sense of purpose and a "raison d'etre" in the language arts curriculum. That's simply because readers theatre is something that engages students and is also something that students want to do. In many ways it is the attachment of *meaning* to repeated readings.

Amy Wingate has been using readers theatre for some time now. Dramatic increases in students' reading fluency and comprehension have been documented through her regular assessment program. Students' interest and attitudes about reading have also changed, in very dramatic ways. By simply allocating a brief section of each day to the practice and performance of readers theatre,

Amy has been able to create a reading program that is both dynamic and purposeful—both in her eyes as well as those of her students.

Figure 5.1 (pp. 66–67) is a plan that Amy uses throughout the school year. Consider this as a possibility for your classroom. You should also feel free to adapt and modify this design in accordance with the dictates of your own classroom reading program and the immediate instructional needs of your students.

On pages 68–70 is the first part of a readers theatre script, "Jack Climbs to the Top of a Very Tall Vegetable and Finds a Very Large Individual with an Attitude Problem," that Amy used with her students during the week outlined in figure 5.1.

Amy's schedule (pp. 66–67) provides her with a variety of instructional options. Most important, it allows her to focus on fluency development using materials that are both motivational and instructionally sound. For Amy, readers theatre is a teaching strategy that is vibrant and exciting—not just for her, but for her students, too!

WHAT OTHERS SAY

In the course of my research for this book I had the opportunity to discuss the value of readers theatre with many educators around the United States. This included teachers who had been using readers theatre as a regular part of their classroom reading program for some time as well as those who were in the initial stages of using readers theatre. As part of my conference presentations, in-service programs, and workshops I chatted with teachers about the role readers theatre had in their classroom curricula. I wanted to know the influence readers theatre had on fluency development as well as other aspects of reading growth and development. Here are a few of the many comments and reactions teachers shared with me:

❖ Lisa (second grade, Atlantic City, New Jersey)—"I really like the way readers theatre helps my students feel more confident and self-assured in their reading. Their reading is smoother and more deliberate."

❖ Sandy (third grade, Chicago, Illinois)—"It was tough at first—finding the time to use it in my room. But, when I saw the changes that were taking place, in just the first six weeks, I knew I had to make it a permanent part of my reading program."

❖ Mark (fifth grade, Austin, Texas)—"For me, readers theatre is all about helping kids read with passion and excitement. I've also found it to be an excellent way to help them improve their comprehension, too."

❖ Sarah (first grade, Erie, Pennsylvania)—"I wish I had discovered readers theatre years ago. The positive changes in my students is absolutely phenomenal. They really feel good about what they're doing in reading. And, they can see their own growth, too."

❖ Amy (fourth grade, Albuquerque, New Mexico)—"My students love readers theatre for a number of reasons. They often remark how they can see changes in their own reading (e.g., fluency) after just a couple of sessions with readers theatre. Their motivation levels are high, too!"

❖ Clarice (third grade, Murfreesboro, Tennessee)—"I truly believe that readers theatre has had a positive effect on my students' fluency development. In addition, they understand more and they read more. What more could I ask for?"

❖ Richard (fourth grade, Orlando, Florida)—"I was very reluctant to add readers theatre to my very crowded schedule. But a friend convinced me that I should. And I've never looked back. The changes are so incredible. Students read with confidence, they read with assurance, and, best of all, they read with excellent comprehension."

❖ Rosanna (sixth grade, Grand Junction, Colorado)—"I had a classroom full of reluctant readers until I introduced them to readers theatre. Now they can't get enough readers theatre because, they too, can see some of its benefits."

❖ Brandi (second grade, Osage Beach, Missouri)—"Readers theatre has been a life-saver for me and my students. Their fluency levels have skyrocketed and so have their comprehension levels. It's been a wonderful addition to my classroom."

❖ Cassie (third grade, Las Vegas, Nevada)—"I love readers theatre! I'd always worried about how I was going to teach fluency to my students . . . one more thing to add to the curriculum. But, readers theatre helped me teach fluency in a way that students enjoyed and that I could schedule fairly easily."

Many teachers are aware of the influence of readers theatre on students. They believe that reading instruction should mirror reading "in the real world." These teachers have seen incredible growth and fantastic changes in the literacy growth of students when readers theatre is made a regular part of students' interactions with literature. Attitudes are changed and interest is heightened (for students and teachers alike). Most important, fluency development becomes a normal and natural part of daily reading instruction.

Figure 5.1. Planning for Readers Theatre

(Amy Wingate—Fourth Grade)

Saturday/Sunday

1. Select an appropriate script ("Jack Climbs to the Top of a Very Tall Vegetable and Finds a Very Large Individual with an Attitude Problem") from the teacher resource book *Frantic Frogs and Other Frankly Fractured Folktales for Readers Theatre* by Anthony D. Fredericks (Westport, CT: Teacher Ideas Press, 1993).

Monday

1. Duplicate six copies (five student copies and one teacher copy) of the selected script.

2. Review the nature and purpose of readers theatre with the class.

3. Introduce the script to the class through an expressive and animated read-aloud presentation.

4. Assign the roles of the five characters (Jack, Mother, Cow, Giant, Narrator) to selected students.

Tuesday

1. Students practice their parts during free time or paired reading time.

2. Notices are sent home to parents about the readers theatre performance taking place on Friday afternoon.

3. Students are allowed to take their scripts home to practice as part of their homework assignments.

Wednesday

1. Students practice their parts during free time or paired reading time.

2. Students are provided with opportunities (away from the rest of the class) to do one or more practice "run-throughs" of the script.

3. Students are allowed to take their scripts home to practice as part of their homework assignments.

Thursday

1. Students practice their parts during free time or paired reading time.

2. Students participate in a final "dress rehearsal" of the script.

3. Students are allowed to take their scripts home one last time to practice as part of their homework assignments.

Friday

1. Students are invited to perform their script for the other members of the class (and a small audience of parents).

2. The performance is videotaped (and will be shared with colleagues in other fourth-grade classrooms).

3. Cookies and punch are served at a post-production party.

4. Students are engaged in a post-production discussion about the script and the way in which it was shared with the entire class.

Saturday/Sunday

1. Select another script ("Rapunzel Gets a Really Lousy Hairdo") from *Frantic Frogs and Other Frankly Fractured Folktales for Readers Theatre* for the following week's production.

JACK CLIMBS TO THE TOP OF A VERY TALL VEGETABLE AND FINDS A VERY LARGE INDIVIDUAL WITH AN ATTITUDE PROBLEM

STAGING: The narrator sits on a stool in front of the characters. The characters may be seated in chairs or standing.

Jack	Mother	Cow		Giant	
X	X	X		X	
				Narrator	
				X	

NARRATOR: You all probably remember the story about Jack and his encounters with a former NBA basketball player who just happened to live at the top of a very tall bean plant. Now the writers who told you that story would have you believe that this very tall person who lived at the top of the very tall bean plant had nothing better to do with his time than eat unsuspecting little boys who just happened to climb to the top of that very tall bean plant looking for a bunch of gold to take home to their poor starving mothers who lived around the bottom of that very tall plant. Well, it is true that giants are known far and wide for their ability to nibble, chew, and chomp on little boys. However, the version you heard of that story is not the real story - the real story is the one that you're going to see right now. So, here goes.

JACK: [excited] Hey, mom, guess what I did. I went down to the marketplace with our cow Bessie and sold her to this nice used car salesman for a handful of cactus seeds.

NARRATOR: [to the audience] Now, it should begin to become apparent that Jack was not the brightest kid around. For, as everyone knows, you can't get cactus seeds from a used car salesman. But, after all, this *is* a fairy tale so why don't we all just pretend?

MOTHER: [angry] You dodo! What do you mean you traded our best cow, in fact, our only cow, for a handful of stupid seeds from some used car salesman.

COW: [to audience] Yeah, think how I feel. I've just spent the last ten years of my life giving this family some of the best milk ever produced in six counties, and this dumb kid just hauls me off to the marketplace, gets taken in by some smooth talking salesman, and trades me for a bunch of cactus seeds. Talk about feeling bad!

MOTHER: [still angry] Jack, you take these stupid cactus seeds, go back down to the stupid marketplace, find that stupid salesman, and get our stupid cow back.

COW: [to the audience] See what I mean. I still can't get any respect around here.

JACK: [lightly] Okay, Mom, I'll do it first thing tomorrow. In the meantime why don't you just throw these seeds out the window and let's see what happens.

69

NARRATOR: I'm sorry, folks, but we're going to have to stop the story right here. In the first place, since these folks live in the mountains there's no way those cactus seeds are going to sprout. As you know, cacti (that's the plural of cactus) only grows in hot, dry areas like deserts. In the second place, imagine what would happen if that cactus actually *did* grow one thousand feet tall. I mean, don't you think Jack would have a really tough time trying to climb to the top of that enormous plant? Talk about getting stuck in a story! It looks like your friendly neighborhood narrator is going to have to save the day once again and change some of the dialogue so that we can continue on with the story. So, here goes.

JACK: [amazed] Oh, how amazing. Those stupid cactus seeds have now magically turned into some stupid bean seeds. Gosh, isn't that narrator amazing?

MOTHER: Yes, and now I can throw those stupid bean seeds out the window and we can continue on with this story.

NARRATOR: Mother throws the bean seeds out the window, they grow about five thousand feet tall during the night, and now it's the next morning.

Excerpted from *Frantic Frogs and Other Frankly Fractured Folktales for Readers Theatre* by Anthony D. Fredericks (Westport, CT: Teacher Ideas Press, 1993), 50–52.

PART II

READERS THEATRE: A CLOSER LOOK

CHAPTER 6

Getting Started with Readers Theatre

Classroom teachers and university researchers recognize the significance and importance of a balanced reading program (Freppon & Dahl 1998; Strickland 1995; Weaver 1998). In a balanced reading program the following elements are integrated into a literacy effort that is well coordinated for all students.

A Balanced Reading Program

Reading Aloud

Reading aloud introduces children to quality literature in a pleasing and comfortable format.

Shared Book Experience

The shared book experience is a cooperative learning activity in which a favorite book is read by the teacher and reread independently by students.

Guided Reading

Guided reading involves a teacher and a small group of students who read a book together for a specific purpose (e.g., making inferences, mental imagery).

Individualized Reading

In individualized reading the teacher matches each student to an appropriate book and invites each student to work at his or her own pace on material suited to individual needs.

Paired Reading

Paired reading allows children the opportunity to work with a partner or buddy. Each pair of students can read the same book together and share appropriate reading strategies or interpretations.

Sustained Silent Reading

Sustained silent reading is that time of the instructional day when everyone—including the teacher—simply reads for an extended period of time.

Language Exploration

Language exploration encourages children to become involved in a wide range of literacy extensions related to a single book or reading in general. These may include discussions, writing, art, music, a range of "hands-on, minds-on" activities, and readers theatre.

Reading and Writing

As children listen and respond to a wide variety of literature, they come in contact with models of efficient writing. These models serve as springboards for the writing children can do in the classroom.

READERS THEATRE IN CONTEXT

It is important to emphasize that readers theatre is not a method for the teaching of reading. Rather, it is part of a larger organizational framework in which teachers make informed decisions about the instructional practices that are best suited for individual students or groups of students at any one time. Readers theatre is part of a decision-making process that recognizes that good teaching requires "doing the right thing in the right way and at the right time in response to problems posed by particular people in particular places on particular occasions" (Garrison 1997, 271). In other words, no two teaching situations will ever be the same, and good teachers of reading are eclectic teachers of reading. As teachers, it is up to us to select the practices and procedures that will have the greatest impact on selected students at selected times.

This book is designed to offer a plethora of strategies, activities, and ideas from which reading teachers can integrate readers theatre into their overall reading program—an integration that will result in higher levels of fluency, increased levels of comprehension, heightened levels of vocabulary, and a deeper appreciation of reading as a "personal act of involvement" (Fredericks 2008b). No two teachers will use these ideas in the same way, nor should they. You are invited to pick and choose or mix and match the suggestions and projects that meet the immediate needs of your students at specific times of the school year. By the same token, you are encouraged to modify, adapt, or alter various ideas within this book to address the changing dynamics of your classroom as well as of your students. In many ways, effective teachers of reading are "thoughtfully adaptive" (Duffy & Hoffman

1999). The underlying theme here is that teachers are professional decision makers, and it is hoped that the ideas within these pages will provide them with the tools necessary to make informed reading instruction decisions according to students' needs and the evolving nature of their classrooms.

It is also important to remember that readers theatre is one element in the overall reading program. A balanced reading program is one in which sufficient attention is devoted to each of several components (e.g., reading aloud, guided reading, sustained silent reading, language exploration, etc.) on a daily basis. The individual time frames for those components will vary from classroom to classroom depending on the philosophy of the school or district, daily time schedules, the reading curriculum, and personal preferences.

INTRODUCING READERS THEATRE TO STUDENTS

Ever since I wrote my first book of readers theatre scripts—*Frantic Frogs and Other Frankly Fractured Folktales for Readers Theatre* (1993)—I have been amazed by and delighted with the incredible response readers theatre has generated among educators across the country. Teachers in urban, suburban, and rural schools have all told me of the incredible power of readers theatre as a regular feature of their language arts or reading curricula. In the teacher in-service programs I conduct and conference workshops I lead on readers theatre, I continue to receive rave reviews of readers theatre as a way of helping students take an active role in the reading process. Many teachers have commented on improved levels of motivation and heightened participation in all aspects of the reading curriculum when readers theatre has been added to students' daily literacy activities.

However, readers theatre is not something you just "drop into" the curriculum one day and expect students to enthusiastically embrace it. It must be introduced to students on a gradual basis—over the course of several days or several weeks—to achieve maximum impact. Of course no two teachers will introduce readers theatre in exactly the same way. What follows is an instructional plan of action that allows for a great deal of latitude and variation depending on how your reading or language arts program is organized as well as the specific time constraints of your classroom schedule. Feel free to make any necessary adjustments or modifications in the schedule to suit your personal philosophy or the specific instructional needs of your students.

My experience, as well as that of many teachers, is that students need to transition through four stages in order for readers theatre to become a viable component of the overall literacy program. These four stages follow:

- **Introduction.** This is the stage at which students are first introduced to readers theatre. In cases where most of the students in your class have been using readers theatre in previous grades, this stage can be eliminated.

- **Familiarization.** In this stage students become comfortable with the concept of readers theatre. They begin to understand its value as an instructional tool as well as its worth in helping them become accomplished and fluent readers.

- **Practice.** Here students are offered a variety of ways in which to practice readers theatre in authentic situations. Students begin to see positive growth and development in both reading fluency and comprehension.

- **Integration.** This stage provides students with regular and systematic opportunities to use readers theatre as a significant element in other aspects of the reading program (e.g., guided reading, literature circles) as well as other subject areas (e.g., science, social studies).

What follows are some suggested instructional activities and presentations to share with your students. These suggestions are general in nature and can be easily incorporated into one or more lesson plans. Again, depending on the dynamics of your overall classroom reading program, the lessons may last for as little as 10 minutes or as much as one hour.

1. **Introduction** (suggested duration: 1–3 days)

    A.   Select a prepared readers theatre script. Choose one of the 16 scripts from this book or from any other readers theatre collection of scripts. (I have frequently found it best to select a script that is humorous in nature so that students can see all the fun that can be part of this technique.) Duplicate sufficient copies of the script for every member of the class.

    B.   Distribute the scripts to students. Tell students that a readers theatre script is exactly like a script used by actors in television, the movies, or plays. The only difference is that in readers theatre the lines don't have to be memorized. Nevertheless, they still have to be read with the same level of enthusiasm and emotion that professional actors use.

    C.   Alert students to the fact that readers theatre will help them improve their individual levels of fluency. Define fluency for students ("smooth reading") and invite them to discuss examples of fluent reading (people making speeches, actors and actresses delivering their lines, etc.).

    D.   Identify and discuss the various printed elements of the script. Identify the narrator, the staging instructions, how the various actor parts are designated, any emotional suggestions noted for specific characters, and other features.

    E.   Invite students to silently read through the script on their own. You may wish to use the script as part of a guided reading lesson. Afterward, ask students to share what they noted in the script (e.g., a narrator, a different style of writing, short parts and long parts). Record students' observations on the chalkboard and plan time to discuss them.

    F.   Use the script as a read-aloud for your students. Tell students that you are going to model how a readers theatre script should be read. Inform them that you will also be modeling fluent and expressive reading. You will add emotion to certain parts and will maintain a consistent rate throughout the reading, as well. Invite students to listen carefully to this initial reading.

    G.   After reading through the script, invite students to discuss what they heard. How did your reading differ from other read-alouds in the classroom? How was it similar? What did they enjoy about your reading? How might they have presented the script? Record their observations on the chalkboard.

    H.   As appropriate, show students another prepared readers theatre script. Invite them to identify selected elements of the script (narrator, specific characters, staging directions, etc.). Make sure students understand that most readers theatre scripts follow a fairly standard format.

2. **Familiarization** (suggested duration: 1 week)

    Before engaging students in this stage you may wish to select 8 to 10 lines or passages from a forthcoming script. It is suggested that these lines or passages come from the beginning of the script and that they be representative of most (if not all) of the characters (including any narrator(s)). Record these passages on cardboard sentence strips (using block printing or a word processing program).

Here are some sample sentence strips from the beginning of the readers theatre script "The Gingerbread Man" (see part III):

NARRATOR 1	Once upon a time there was a Little Old Woman . . . .

LITTLE OLD WOMAN	That's me!

NARRATOR 2	. . . and a Little Old Man.

LITTLE OLD MAN	That's me!

NARRATOR 1	Well, they both lived alone in a little old house in the middle of the little old woods. They were very lonely, so one day the Little Old Woman decided to make a Gingerbread Boy.

NARRATOR 2	So she rolled out some gingerbread, sprinkled it with cinnamon, used some raisins for his eyes, and made his mouth out of rose-colored sugar. She put him on a pan and put him in the oven.

NARRATOR 1	After a time she opened the oven door and took out the pan.

LITTLE OLD WOMAN	That's what I did—I took out the pan!

LITTLE OLD MAN	Yes, she took out the pan.

After creating the necessary sentence strips, engage students in the following sequence of activities:

A. Select a prepared readers theatre script (one from this book, such as "The Gingerbread Man," or any other collection of scripts). Record the script on audiotape (you may wish to alter your voice slightly for each of the characters or enlist the aid of some other teachers, or parents, to help you record the script). Make sure this recording of the script is fluent and smooth (practice several times if necessary).

B. Provide students with copies of the selected script. Point out, once more, how a readers theatre script is organized (e.g., narrator, individual characters, etc.). Tell them that they will listen to a reading of the script on an audiotape.

C. Play the recording for students. Invite them to listen carefully for the smooth and fluent reading. Encourage them, as appropriate, to follow along by pointing to each of the words as they hear it.

D. You may wish to repeat the sequence above, particularly if you are using this sequence with a group of struggling readers who may need some additional reinforcement and assistance.

E. Provide an opportunity for students to discuss what they heard, the intonation exhibited by the readers, the smoothness of their delivery, or any other aspects of the recording. You may wish to record these observations on the chalkboard or a sheet of newsprint.

F. Invite the class (or group) to read through the entire script chorally. You should also participate in this choral reading so that students have a positive model and an appropriate support system for their oral reading. At this stage, it would be appropriate to emphasize the emotions that selected characters may bring to their parts (e.g., anger, disgust, happiness).

G. After the choral reading, randomly distribute the sentence strips to selected students. Inform the students that they will now become the characters in the play. Invite the students to stand in a line. Point to each character (using the sequence in the script) and invite each student to read his or her selected passage.

H. Invite other students to listen and comment (in a positive way) about the presentation of the first part of the script.

I. Distribute the sentence strips to another group of students and invite them to line up and recite the passages as the previous group did. Again, it would be appropriate to discuss the nature of the presentation in a supportive atmosphere.

J. (optional) Play the recorded version of the script again for the students. Invite them to make any additional comments.

3. **Practice** (suggested duration: 1–2 weeks)

A. Select, duplicate, and distribute a prepared script to all the students in your class. *Note:* At this particular stage I have frequently given students a selection of possible scripts from which the entire class makes a single choice. This gives students a sense of ownership over the script, which ultimately results in a heightened level of motivation.

B. Divide the class into pairs or triads of students. Invite students to share the script in their small groups. Students may wish to read the script silently, after which they may discuss the story line, characters, plot, or other elements. Students may also elect to read certain sections to each other, not only to practice fluent reading, but also to get a "feel" for the story.

C. Assign roles. I like to assign one student from each of the small groups to a character in the script. (If there are, for example, six characters, I make sure that students are initially divided into six small groups). Each character then practices his or her part with the other members of his or her group (for example, the character reads only his or her own lines to group members, who assist with any difficult words or comment on the fluency of the reading).

D. When students have had sufficient practice, arrange them according to the staging directions for that script.

E. Invite the assigned students to read through the script just as they practiced it. Invite others students to listen to the presentation. After the script is completed, discuss how it might be improved the next time.

F. (optional) Reassign roles to different students in the class. Divide the class into small groups and repeat the sequence as described above.

4. **Integration** (suggested duration: remainder of the school year or remainder of the unit)

   A.   Select a prepared readers theatre script (one from this book or any other collection of scripts). Assign roles to selected students and distribute copies of the scripts to those students. You may wish to use two or three separate scripts—each distributed to a different group of students in the class.

   B.   Invite students to practice their assigned parts in preparation for a production later on. Students should be provided with practice time in class and should also be encouraged to practice their respective parts at home (see the parent letters in this chapter, pages 88–91).

   C.   Schedule a day and time when students will present their scripts to others in the class. This initial presentation should be kept as an in-class one to allay any fears students may have about presenting to an unfamiliar group of individuals. Ask students if they would like to invite their parents to attend this presentation.

   D.   After presenting the initial script, invite students to select other prepared scripts for a more formal presentation (see chapter 8).

   E.   Invite students to create their own readers theatre scripts from self-selected literature in the classroom or school library (see chapter 7). Make this process a normal part of your writing program or a basic element of a writer's workshop. After students have created their own scripts, provide them with opportunities to present them to appropriate audiences, including classrooms at a grade level above or below yours.

   F.   Consider the implementation of readers theatre as a fundamental element in literature circles. After students have engaged in a discussion about a self-selected book, invite them to develop the book into a readers theatre script that may become a permanent part of the classroom library.

   G.   Students may wish to use readers theatre as part of a thematic unit. According to Meinbach et al., "a thematic approach to learning combines structured, sequential, and well-organized strategies, activities, children's literature, and materials used to expand a particular concept" (2000, 10). Readers theatre has the advantage of offering youngsters a creative and dynamic way to utilize their reading abilities in a productive and engaging way. By integrating readers theatre into thematic units, you will help students gain a deeper appreciation of the role of reading (and reading fluency) in their overall literacy development.

   H.   Use prepared scripts (for example, from *Nonfiction Readers Theatre for Beginning Readers* by Anthony D. Fredericks) or student-created scripts as part of your content area instruction. Readers theatre has been shown to stimulate curiosity (when used in advance of a content area unit) and promote enthusiasm (when used as part of an instructional unit), particularly when incorporated into science and social studies (Fredericks 2007).

   I.   Readers theatre can be effectively incorporated into guided reading activities in any classroom. The three critical and interrelated stages of guided reading (before reading, during reading, and after reading) offer you and your students unique opportunities to weave readers theatre into the overall reading curriculum. Imagine the thrill and excitement of students using a self-designed script as the reading selection in a guided reading group! Readers theatre holds the promise of helping students in a guided reading group understand and appreciate the richness of language, the ways in which to interpret that language, and how language can be a powerful vehicle for the comprehension and appreciation of different forms of literature (Fredericks 2001).

Following are two suggested schedules that you may wish to use with readers theatre. The first is designed for students who have not been previously exposed to readers theatre. The second is an abbreviated schedule designed for students who have some familiarity or practice with readers theatre. As with the suggestions above, please feel free to adjust these schedules in accordance with the time demands of your classroom reading program or the specific needs of your students.

1. Schedule for Readers Theatre (for Students New to Readers Theatre)

	Monday	Tuesday	Wednesday	Thursday	Friday
Week 1	Selection of script(s); teacher read-through	Listen to audiotape of script(s).	Distribution of script(s) to students. First read-through	Assignment of parts; second read- through	Group practice
Week 2	Individual or group practice	Individual or group practice	Work with teacher as necessary	Individual or group practice	Assess fluency rate of 4–6 students
Week 3	Work with teacher as necessary	Individual or group practice	Production and distribution of printed programs	Performance	Assess fluency rate of 4–6 students

2. Schedule for Readers Theatre (for Students with Prior Readers Theatre Experience)

	Monday	Tuesday	Wednesday	Thursday	Friday
Week 1	Selection of script(s); characters are assigned; scripts are distributed.	Students practice their parts. Teacher models as necessary.	Students practice their parts. Practice may be in groups and/or for homework.	Students practice their parts. Dress rehearsal or "dry run."	Students perform for the class or another audience.

PLANNING FOR READERS THEATRE

Pages 82–87 are "plans" for scheduling readers theatre into the reading activities of your classroom. The arrows indicate that each group will be doing the same thing. Depending on the amount of time available for reading instruction as well as the time necessary for other subject areas, you may wish to modify or adjust these schedules accordingly. The three time frames are:

1. Two hours and 45 minutes available for reading instruction each day

2. Two 45-minute blocks of time available for reading instruction each day

3. One 45-minute block of time available for reading instruction each day

THE HOMEWORK CONNECTION

For me, readers theatre is one of the most exciting and dynamic reading activities for any elementary classroom. Thousands of teachers all over the country have also discovered a new vitality and new enthusiasm for reading when readers theatre has been incorporated into the regular reading program. Teachers are enthused and children and excited about this "active engagement in text."

You can help extend those learning opportunities for your students by inviting parents to become part of the entire experience. The informational letters in the handouts on pages 88–91 provide parents and caregivers with valuable information about this addition to your reading curriculum. In addition, students can practice their fluency skills in a supportive environment (just imagine dad taking on the role of the Big Bad Wolf) that extends and expands readers theatre in new directions and dimensions.

ONE MORE THING

You will discover, as I have, that there are innumerable ways of introducing your students to readers theatre. The suggestions offered in this chapter are just that: suggestions. Modify these ideas and adjust these schedules to suit your own instructional objectives or program guidelines. Invite students to make suggestions about when and where readers theatre could be integrated into the curriculum. Work with your colleagues at your grade level to make readers theatre a regular and systematic element in the overall literacy development of youngsters.

I think you will discover, as have thousands of other teachers, that readers theatre is, and can be, a touch of literary magic for your classroom. Be creative, inventive, and experimental, and you will soon discover enormous possibilities for teaching this most valuable reading skill: fluency.

SAMPLE 1

2 hours and 45 minutes for reading instruction

Groups →	A	B	C	D
9:00–9:15	Opening Daily news			
9:15–9:45	Shared book experience			
9:45–10:15	Guided reading	Individualized reading Paired reading	**Readers theatre** Reading and writing	Individualized reading
10:15–10:30	Reading aloud			
10:30–11:00	**Readers theatre**	Guided reading	Individualized reading Paired reading	**Readers theatre** Reading and writing
11:00–11:30	Individualized reading	**Readers theatre**	Reading and writing	Paired reading
11:30–11:45	Sustained silent reading			

SAMPLE 2

2 hours and 45 minutes for reading instruction

Groups →	A	B	C	D
9:00–9:15	Opening Daily news			
9:15–9:45	Shared book experience			
9:45–10:15	**Readers theatre** Reading and writing	Guided reading	Individualized reading	Individualized reading Paired reading
10:15–10:30	Reading aloud			
10:30–11:00	Reading and writing	Individualized reading	**Readers theatre**	Readers theatre
11:00–11:30	Individualized reading Paired reading	**Readers theatre** Reading and writing	Paired reading	Guided reading
11:30–11:45	Sustained silent reading			

From *Building Fluency with Readers Theatre: Motivational Strategies, Successful Lessons and Dynamic Scripts to Develop Fluency, Comprehension, Writing, and Vocabulary* by Anthony D. Fredericks. Westport, CT: Teacher Ideas Press. Copyright © 2008.

SAMPLE 3

Two 45-minute blocks of time for reading instruction

Groups →	A	B	C	D
9:15–9:30	Shared book experience			
9:30–10:00	Guided Reading	Individualized reading Paired reading	**Readers theatre** Reading and writing	Individualized reading
10:00– 10:45	(Content area subject)			
10:45–11:00	Reading aloud			
11:00–11:30	**Readers theatre**	Guided reading	Individualized reading Paired reading	**Readers theatre** Reading and writing

SAMPLE 4

Two 45-minute blocks of time for reading instruction

Groups →	A	B	C	D
9:15–9:30	Reading aloud ⟶			
9:30–10:00	**Readers theatre** Reading and writing	Guided reading	Individualized reading	Individualized reading
10:00–10:45	(Content area subject) ⟶			
10:45–11:00	Sustained silent reading ⟶			
11:00–11:30	Individualized reading Paired reading	**Readers theatre** Reading and writing	**Readers theatre** Paired reading	Guided reading

SAMPLE 5

One 45-minute block of time for reading instruction

Groups →	A	B	C	D
9:15–9:30	Reading aloud			
9:30–10:00	Guided reading	Readers theatre	Guided reading	Readers theatre

NOTE: None of the groups (A, B C, D) listed in sample 5 is permanent. They are organized and arranged according to students' needs and abilities. Some may exist for a few days; others may exist for two or three weeks. The grouping paradigms illustrated above are not the traditional arrangement of "High," "Average," and "Low" reading groups. Rather, groups are formed and reformed in a variety of patterns according to the dynamics of the reading program and the specific instructional needs of children.

SAMPLE 6

One 45-minute block of time for reading instruction

	Monday	**Tuesday**	**Wednesday**	**Thursday**	**Friday**
Reading aloud		15 min.		15 min.	
Shared book experience				15 min.	
Guided reading	30 min.		15 min.		30 min.
Individualized reading		15 min.			
Paired reading			15 min.		
Sustained silent reading	15 min.				15 min.
Readers theatre		15 min.		15 min.	
Reading and writing			15 min.		

From *Building Fluency with Readers Theatre: Motivational Strategies, Successful Lessons and Dynamic Scripts to Develop Fluency, Comprehension, Writing, and Vocabulary* by Anthony D. Fredericks. Westport, CT: Teacher Ideas Press. Copyright © 2008.

LETTER 1

Dear Parent(s)/Guardian(s):

We are about to begin an exciting new part of our classroom reading program: readers theatre. Readers theatre is a teaching strategy that helps students become better communicators and better readers. Readers theatre encourages students to read with expression and enthusiasm. It helps them become fluent readers—readers who read smoothly and effortlessly.

Readers theatre has been used in many classrooms across the country. It helps students understand characters and their feelings. It helps them understand how stories are developed. Most important, it has been shown to be a positive teaching tool that fosters comprehension growth in all students. We are excited about the possibilities for your child.

Readers theatre is like a play—however, unlike a play, there are no lines to memorize. Students must, however, practice their lines so that their reading of those lines (during a performance, for example) will be smooth and effortless. Your child's participation in readers theatre will encourage clear projection, good expression, and fluency in reading.

I would like to encourage your support of this part of our classroom reading program. Work with your child in practicing his/her lines. Read a script to your child and invite your child to read the script to you. Praise your child when he/she reads smoothly and clearly. Plan time to listen to your child. Provide opportunities for your child to read to other family members.

Readers theatre is an exciting classroom activity that will assist your child in becoming the best reader possible. I welcome your involvement and support of this valuable learning tool.

Thank you in advance for your support.

Sincerely,

LETTER 2

Dear Parent(s)/Guardian(s):

Reading stories to your children is a most valuable activity. When children listen to adults read, it helps them develop an appreciation for written material and for the ideas and thoughts that books can convey. Many experts in the field of reading have determined that parents who read to their children on a regular basis are more likely to have children who are good readers.

Reading aloud is perhaps the most important way you can guide your child toward reading success. You can open up whole new worlds of adventure and discovery that cannot be found anywhere else, including TV! Children who have been read to will undoubtedly be eager to read for themselves because they know the pleasures to be found in books. Here are some suggestions:

1. Before reading to your child, practice reading aloud by yourself the first few times to feel more comfortable.

2. Establish a relaxed atmosphere with no radio, TV, or other distractions. Try setting aside a family reading time when everyone reads.

3. Encourage your child to stop to ask questions or to point out details. This shows that your child is interested in what you are reading.

4. You may want to stop from time to time in your reading to ask questions about some of the characters or events in the story. Ask questions like, "Why do you think he/she did that?"

5. As you read a story, record it on cassette tape. Later, your child can listen to the story again just by playing the tape independently.

Sincerely,

LETTER 3

Dear Parent(s)/Guardian(s):

Learning to read is one of the most valuable skills your child can ever learn. One practice that helps children continue on the road to reading success is for parents to set aside a special time each day to read with their children. This sharing time is important because it demonstrates to your child that reading can be fun, exciting, and informative. Best of all, when parents and children read together they have a special sharing time—available in no other activity. This time together not only helps your child develop a positive relationship toward books, but also reinforces the important emotional bond between parent and child. Plan to take a few moments each day to share the joy of literature with your child. Here are some ideas:

1. Give your child plenty of opportunities to choose the reading materials you read together. Let him/her pick books based on special interests or hobbies.

2. Read aloud with lots of expression. You may wish to take on the role of one of the characters in a book and adjust your voice accordingly.

3. As you read an old familiar story to your child, occasionally leave out a word and ask your child to supply the missing word or a synonym.

4. Every once in a while do some shared reading. You read one paragraph to your child, and your child reads one paragraph to you . . . and so on and so on.

5. Make reading a regular part of your family activities. Be sure to take books along on family outings or trips. Read to your child every chance you get.

Sincerely,

 From *Building Fluency with Readers Theatre: Motivational Strategies, Successful Lessons and Dynamic Scripts to Develop Fluency, Comprehension, Writing, and Vocabulary* by Anthony D. Fredericks. Westport, CT: Teacher Ideas Press. Copyright © 2008.

LETTER 4

Dear Parent(s)/Guardian(s):

Your child has been practicing for a readers theatre production of the following script: _____

Your child's involvement in this production will help improve his/her reading comprehension and fluency (smooth reading). I would like to ask that you support your child's involvement in this production by listening to him/her practice at home. Plan time when your child can read his/her part aloud to you. Listen carefully and closely. Praise your child when he/she does well and encourage your child when he/she needs some assistance.

Here is a checklist of things you can listen for as your child practices his/her part(s) in this production. You may wish to share some of these with your child:

My child:

_____   Is familiar with the script.

_____   Is able to read the material comfortably.

_____   Knows his/her own place in the script.

_____   Demonstrates confidence.

_____   Demonstrates enthusiasm in his/her reading.

_____   Reads with expression.

_____   Reads smoothly.

_____   Uses actions to enhance the reading.

_____   Reads at a good pace.

_____   Enjoys his/her performance.

Sincerely,

CHAPTER 7

Finding and Creating Readers Theatre Scripts

When I share my passion for readers theatre in teacher workshops and conference presentations throughout the country, I am frequently asked, "Where can I find some readers theatre scripts?" Although I'm often tempted to tell them about my own collections of readers theatre scripts (see below), I also want teachers to know about the wide array of other resources at their disposal. In short, there is an incredible collection of readers theatre books and resources available for teachers—all with dynamic, exciting, and powerful readers theatre scripts for every grade level, every curricular area, and every classroom.

SCRIPT SOURCES

Readers Theatre Scripts (Teacher Resource Books)

The following list includes some of the best published collections of readers theatre scripts. All can be ordered online or can be found in many bookstores and libraries. Check with your school librarian to see if she or he has any of these books in the teacher resource collection. If not, please suggest that some of these be ordered for addition to the library collection.

As you will note, a few publishers specialize in readers theatre books for elementary teachers. These publishers have made a conscious attempt to provide teachers, librarians, and reading specialists with an assortment of quality-based readers theatre books that can be used throughout the reading curriculum. You may wish to check out these publishers first:

- Teacher Ideas Press—www.teacherideaspress.com

- Scholastic—www.scholastic.com

- Shepard Publications—www.shepardpub.com

Following are some of the most popular teacher resource books with ready-to-use scripts for any classroom or library.

Barchers, S., and M. Ruscoe. *Against All Odds*. Westport, CT: Teacher Ideas Press, 2008.

———. *Fifty Fabulous Fables: Beginning Readers Theatre*. Westport, CT: Teacher Ideas Press, 1997.

———. *Judge for Yourself*. Westport, CT: Teacher Ideas Press, 2004.

Barchers, S., and C. R. Pfeffinger. *More Readers Theatre for Beginning Readers*. Westport, CT: Teacher Ideas Press, 2006.

———. *Multicultural Folktales: Readers Theatre for Elementary Students*. Westport, CT: Teacher Ideas Press, 2000.

———. *Readers Theatre for Beginning Readers*. Westport, CT: Teacher Ideas Press, 1993.

———. *Scary Readers Theatre*. Westport, CT: Teachers Ideas Press, 1994.

Barnes, J. W. *Sea Songs*. Westport, CT: Teacher Ideas Press, 2004.

Bauer, C. F. *Presenting Reader's Theatre*. New York: H. W.Wilson, 1991.

Black, A. N. *Born Storytellers*. Westport, CT: Teacher Ideas Press, 2005.

———. *Readers Theatre for Middle School Boys*. Westport, CT: Teacher Ideas Press, 2008.

Braun, W. *A Reader's Theatre Treasury of Stories*. Calgary, AB: Braun and Braun, 2000.

Charlesworth, L. *Plays Around the Year*. New York: Scholastic, 1994.

Criscoe, B. L., and P.J. Lanasa. *Fairy Tales for Two Readers*. Westport, CT: Teacher Ideas Press, 1995.

Dixon, N., A. Davies, C. and Politano. *Learning with Readers Theatre: Building Connections*. Winnipeg, MB: Peguis Publishers, 1996.

Fry, E. *25 Mini-Plays: World History*. New York: Scholastic, 2000.

Garner, J. *Wings of Fancy: Using Readers Theatre to Study Fantasy Genre*. Westport, CT: Teacher Ideas Press, 2006

Georges, C., and C. Cornett. *Reader's Theatre*. Buffalo, NY: D.O.K. Publishers, 1990.

Haven, K. *Great Moments in Science: Experiments and Readers Theatre*. Westport, CT: Teacher Ideas Press, 1996.

Jenkins, D. R. *Just Deal with It*. Westport, CT: Teacher Ideas Press, 2004.

Johnson, T. D., and D. R. Louis. *Bringing It All Together: A Program for Literacy*. Portsmouth, NH: Heinemann, 1990.

Kroll, J. L. *Simply Shakespeare*. Westport, CT: Teacher Ideas Press, 2003.

Latrobe, K. H., C. Casey, and L. A. Gann. *Social Studies Readers Theatre for Young Adults*. Westport, CT: Teacher Ideas Press, 1991.

Laughlin, M. K., and K.H. Latrobe. *Readers Theatre for Children*. Westport, CT: Teacher Ideas Press, 1990.

Laughlin, M. K., P. T. Black, and K. H. Latrobe. *Social Studies Readers Theatre for Children*. Westport, CT: Teacher Ideas Press, 1991.

Martin, J. M. *12 Fabulously Funny Fairy Tale Plays*. New York: Instructor Books, 2002.

Peterson, C. *Around the World Through Holidays*. Westport, CT: Teacher Ideas Press, 2005.

Pfeffinger, C. R. *Character Counts*. Westport, CT: Teacher Ideas Press, 2003.

———. *Holiday Readers Theatre*. Westport, CT: Teacher Ideas Press, 1994.

Pugliano-Martin, C. *25 Just-Right Plays for Emergent Readers (Grades K–1)*. New York: Scholastic, 1999.

Sanders, J., and N. I. Sanders. *Readers Theatre for African American History*. Westport, CT: Teacher Ideas Press, 2008.

Shepard, A. *Folktales on Stage: Children's Plays for Readers Theatre*. Olympia, WA: Shepard Publications, 2003.

———. *Readers on Stage: Resources for Readers Theatre*. Olympia, WA: Shepard Publications, 2004.

———. *Stories on Stage: Children's Plays for Readers Theatre*. Olympia, WA: Shepard Publications, 2005.

Sloyer, S. *From the Page to the Stage*. Westport, CT: Teacher Ideas Press, 2003.

Smith, C. *Extraordinary Women from American History*. Westport, CT: Teacher Ideas Press, 2003.

Wolf, J. M. *Cinderella Outgrows the Glass Slipper and Other Zany Fractured Fairy Tale Plays*. New York: Scholastic, 2002.

Wolfman, J. *How and Why Stories for Readers Theatre*. Westport, CT: Teacher Ideas Press, 2004.

Worthy, J. *Readers Theatre for Building Fluency: Strategies and Scripts for Making the Most of This Highly Effective, Motivating, and Research-Based Approach to Oral Reading*. New York: Scholastic, 2005.

Readers Theatre Scripts by Anthony D. Fredericks (the Author of This Book)

Fredericks, A. D. *African Legends, Myths and Folktales for Readers Theatre*. Westport, CT: Teacher Ideas Press, 2008.

———. *American Folktales, Legends and Tall Tales for Readers Theatre*. Westport, CT: Teacher Ideas Press, 2008.

———. *Frantic Frogs and Other Frankly Fractured Folktales for Readers Theatre*. Westport, CT: Teacher Ideas Press, 1993.

———. *MORE Frantic Frogs and Other Frankly Fractured Folktales for Readers Theatre*. Westport, CT: Teacher Ideas Press, 2008.

———. *Mother Goose Readers Theatre for Beginning Readers*. Westport, CT: Teacher Ideas Press, 2007.

———. *Nonfiction Readers Theatre for Beginning Readers*. Westport, CT: Teacher Ideas Press, 2007.

———. *Readers Theatre for American History*. Westport, CT: Teacher Ideas Press, 2001.

———. *Science Fiction Readers Theatre*. Westport, CT: Teacher Ideas Press, 2002.

———. *Silly Salamanders and Other Slightly Stupid Stories for Readers Theatre*. Westport, CT: Teacher Ideas Press, 2000.

———. *Songs and Rhymes Readers Theatre for Beginning Readers*. Westport, CT: Teacher Ideas Press, 2008.

———. *Tadpole Tales and Other Totally Terrific Treats for Readers Theatre*. Westport, CT: Teacher Ideas Press, 1997.

Web Sites

The Internet continues to be an excellent source of readers theatre scripts for classroom teachers. Consider the following Web sites to keep your classroom filled with an interesting assembly of scripts for use throughout your reading curriculum and beyond.

http://www.aaronshep.com/rt/

How to use readers theatre, sample scripts from a children's author who specializes in readers theatre, and an extensive list of resources.

http://www.cdli.ca/CITE/langrt.htm

This site has lots of information, in various sections: "What Is Readers Theatre?" "Readers Theatre Scripts," "Writing Scripts," "Recommended Print Resources," and "Recommended On-line Resources."

http://www.teachingheart.net/readerstheater.htm

Here you'll discover lots of plays and scripts to print and read in your classroom or library.

http://literacyconnections.com/readerstheater

There is an incredible number of resources and scripts at this all-inclusive site.

http://scriptsforschools.com/

This site overflows with all sorts of information, resources, and scripts for any classroom teacher looking for up-to-date information.

http://www.readerstheatredigest.com

This site bills itself as "A blog-journal for readers theatre practitioners and interested others."

http://www.readerstheatre.escd.net

This site has more than 150 small poems, stories, and chants for readers theatre.

http://www.proteacher.com/070173.shtml

This is an all-inclusive site at which you'll discover readers theatre scripts as well as an array of fascinating resources for every classroom teacher.

http://www.readers-theatre.com/

Lots of resources, scripts, and information are what you'll find at this dynamic site.

http://www.storycart.com

Storycart's Press's subscription service provides an inexpensive opportunity to have timely scripts delivered to teachers or librarians each month. Each script is created or adapted by well-known writer Suzanne Barchers, author of several readers theatre books (see above).

Professional Organization

This professional organization focuses on the implementation and use of readers theatre in the classroom. Contact this group and ask about its services and resources for teachers.

Institute for Readers Theatre
P.O. Box 421262
San Diego, CA 92142
(858) 277-4274
http://www.readerstheatreinstitute.com

CREATING YOUR OWN READERS THEATRE SCRIPTS

Some of the most interesting scripts for use in any classroom are those created by teachers using literature or books familiar to students. A favorite children's book or story achieves its greatest potency when it is developed into an appropriate readers theatre script and when students are provided with authentic opportunities to "breath life" into the story by taking on the roles of their favorite characters.

Following are some suggestions you may wish to consider in developing your own readers theatre scripts. They are purposely generic in nature and can be used with almost all kinds of reading material. Although the task of creating scripts from relevant literature may appear daunting at first, you will soon discover, as I have, that the process becomes easier the more scripts you write. The first few scripts you write may take longer than expected; however, you will find that the process becomes easier with each script and will soon develop a "routine" that allows you to create classroom scripts efficiently. The bonus, of course, is that students will know that they are engaged in a production that was initiated and developed by their teacher—certainly a positive motivational tool in any reading program.

Select an Appropriate Story

The best stories for readers theatre are those with tight plots and clear endings, distinctive characters, engaging dialogue, and universal themes (e.g., good over evil, love conquers all, logic is more powerful than strength). I have found it to be particularly worthwhile to include a variety of fiction and nonfiction stories—thus illustrating the power of readers theatre as a literacy activity appropriate for all genres of literature. It is not necessary to use an entire book or story; you may wish to focus on a particular scene, a climactic piece of action, or a specific character event.

I also suggest that you consider stories included in your basal reading text. Many of these are just the right length for development into readers theatre scripts. In some series, there may also be examples of readers theatre scripts that can be used as models for your own scripts.

You may also want to involve your students in this selection process. Ask them to name titles of books or stories you have read to them. Which ones would they like to see developed into readers theatre scripts? By starting with books and stories most familiar to students—particularly those stories that have been used as read-alouds—you will be ensuring an emphasis on fluency development. Once you have modeled the fluent reading of a story, students will be able to make connections between your modeling and their own performance of any script.

Read the Story

Read the book or story out loud. This can be done as a regular classroom activity. It is also valuable to read the story to listen for any lapses in the story line or the need for new dialogue for selected characters.

I have found it particularly valuable to read a story or book out loud in front of a mirror. Although I frequently get some strange stares from my dog (and equally appropriate comments from my wife), I have found that this technique helps me tremendously in judging the pace and flow of the story plot as well as focusing on the need to insert or eliminate dialogue to keep the story moving forward. As you read, listen carefully to the dialogue of characters (fiction) or the places in which a character (with accompanying dialogue) could be added to keep the information flowing (nonfiction).

Character Development

When selecting stories, the number of characters is important. I have found that two to six characters works best. For that reason, some minor characters may be eliminated and their dialogue "absorbed" by other characters. On the other hand, one or two brand new characters may need to be developed to facilitate the pace of the story. It is important that the staging area not be crowded with too many characters because the audience will be distracted.

At this point I photocopy the story. Using a magic marker, I begin marking the story with the names of selected characters. I write each character's name directly on the photocopy at a point where I would like him or her to say something. I may use story dialogue or create some new dialogue. The magic marker also allows me to easily eliminate unnecessary dialogue or actions.

At this point it is also necessary to include one or more narrators. A narrator helps to move the action along; he or she provides a "bridge" between various scenes or characters. If you want the audience to know that a scene has shifted or that a character is thinking about something, this is the place to insert a narrator into the script. The main duty of a narrator is to keep the plot moving at a good clip and to provide appropriate insights for the audience.

Drafting the Script

At this point, I have found it advantageous to use a sheet of chart pack paper, a large piece of newsprint, or the overhead projector for the initial draft. Now I begin to rewrite the story using a series of sequential steps, such as the following:

- Rewrite the title (as appropriate).

- Eliminate unnecessary dialogue or minor characters.

- Insert a narrator at strategic points to advance the action or identify specific scenes.

- Add words that describe the tone of voice used by a specific character (e.g., "rapid," "irritated," "confused")

- Underline or boldface the names of characters for easy identification.

- Create new dialogue, characters, or settings to advance the story or produce a humorous situation.

- Consider the few props necessary for the story.

There is no ideal sequence of steps to follow in the design of readers theatre scripts. Each story or book will have its own set of "needs" as it is being developed into an appropriate script.

After the initial (and very messy) draft is sketched out, I begin to transfer the work into a secondary draft on my word processor. This is the time to begin finalizing the dialogue of selected characters and the narrator(s). It is also an opportunity to make sure that the presentation of the script will not be too short or too long (15 minutes is the maximum length for any classroom script).

Questions to Ask

After producing a draft on the computer, there are a few questions I like to ask myself before I can say that the script is complete. Not all of these will be appropriate for every script, but you may wish to consider these as you begin developing favorite books and stories into readers theatre scripts for your students.

- Is there a balance between parts (each character has approximately the same amount of dialogue)?

- Has a narrator been inserted in appropriate places?

- Have students heard the story previously, and are they familiar with the story?

- Is the action logical and sequential?

- Will audience attention and interest be maintained throughout?

- Is the text or dialogue appropriate for the reading levels of designated students?

- Is the script a true representation of the original story?

- Does the script language support and enhance fluent reading?

Following is an example of how a section of a published children's book was adapted and developed into a readers theatre script:

Near One Cattail: Turtles, Logs and Leaping Frogs

by Anthony D. Fredericks

(Nevada City, CA: Dawn Publications, 2005)

Here is a world where tadpoles play,
And crowds of bugs dance through the day,
With lilies and duckweed everywhere,
Some long-legged birds and a crayfish pair.
Among the rushes where herons repose
A fuzzy cattail flowers and grows.

This is the cattail.

The marshy land with a layer of ooze
Was explored by a girl in high-topped shoes.
A quizzical thought crossed her face:
"What creatures live in this bog-boggy place?"

When she looked at the wildlife one by one,
As they skittered and scattered in the noonday sun,
She discovered a kingdom wild and grand,
A web of life in a soggy land.

Excerpted from *Near One Cattail: Turtles, Logs and Leaping Frogs* by Anthony D. Fredericks (© 2005). Used by permission of the author.

Readers Theatre Adaptation of *Near One Cattail: Turtles, Logs and Leaping Frogs*

SAM: Welcome to a special place.

CARRIE: Why is this place special?

SAM: This is a world where tadpoles play, and crowds of bugs dance through the day.

CARRIE: Wow, that does sound special. Tell me more.

TYRONE: Well, there are lilies and duckweed everywhere, some long-legged birds and a crayfish pair.

CARRIE: I think I like this place. What else?

MELISSA: Among the rushes where herons repose, a fuzzy cattail flowers and grows.

CARRIE:	Can anyone visit?
INEZ:	Yes. The marshy land with a layer of ooze was explored by a girl in high-topped shoes.
CARRIE:	What was she thinking?
PETER:	Well, a quizzical thought crossed her face: "What creatures live in this bog-boggy place?"
NARRATOR:	The young girl began to slowly walk through the wetland. She looked at the wildlife one by one, as they skittered and scattered in the noonday sun.
CARRIE:	Did she see anything?
SAM:	Yes. She discovered a kingdom wild and grand.
CARRIE:	I know—it was a web of life in a soggy land!

Worthy (2005) underscores the value of teachers creating readers theatre scripts using books from the classroom library. As she states, "most teachers (and students) eventually find that using children's books in their own classrooms is more satisfying and motivating." She explains that there are two basic categories of children's literature teachers can use in developing appropriate readers theatre scripts: those that can be performed with little or no modification of the text, and those that require reformatting into scripts (see the example above).

Following are two lists of books appropriate for development into readers theatre scripts. These lists are not meant to be all-inclusive, but rather representative samples of appropriate books. As you become more comfortable designing and formatting readers theatre scripts, you will discover other books in your collection, and in the school library, that can be shared with students as both read-alouds and readers theatre productions.

Selected Children's Books Requiring Minimal Rewriting or Scripting

A Light in the Attic by Shel Silverstein

Bringing the Rain to Kapiti Plain by Verna Aardema

Charlie and the Chocolate Factory: A Play by Roald Dahl

Chicka, Chicka, Boom, Boom by Bill Martin Jr.

Cinder-Elly by Francis Minter

Click, Clack, Moo: Cows That Type by Doreen Cronin

Fortunately by Remy Charlip

Gila Monsters Meet You at the Airport by Marjorie Sharmat

I Am Phoenix: Poems for Two Voices by Paul Fleischman

I'm Gonna Like Me by Jamie Lee Curtis

If I Were in Charge of the World by Judith Viorst

Joyful Noise: Poems for Two Voices by Paul Fleischman

New Kid on the Block, The by Jack Prelutsky

Over in the Jungle: A Rainforest Rhyme by Marianne Berkes

Raven: A Trickster Tale from the Pacific Northwest by Gerald McDermott

Sheep in a Jeep by Nancy Shaw

Sheep in a Shop by Nancy Shaw

Sheep on a Ship by Nancy Shaw

The Very Hungry Caterpillar by Eric Carle

Wilfred Gordon McDonald Partridge by Mem Fox

Yo, Yes by Chris Raschka

You Read to Me, I'll Read to You by Maryann Hoberman

Selected Children's Books Requiring Rewriting and Reformatting

Alexander, Who Used to Be Rich Last Sunday by Judith Viorst

Amazing Grace by Mary Hoffman

Amber Brown (series) by Paula Danziger

Boy Who Cried Wolf, The by Freda Littledale

A Chair for My Mother by Vera Williams

The Christmas Miracle of Jonathan Toomey by Susan Wojciechowski

Cinderella by Charles Perrault

The Dinosaurs of Waterhouse Hawkins by Barbara Kerley

The Frog Prince Continued by Jon Scieszka

The Great Kapok Tree by Lynne Cherry

Hattie and the Fox by Mem Fox

Henry's Freedom Box by Ellen Levine

In One Tidepool: Crabs, Snails and Salty Tails by Anthony D. Fredericks

Jabuti the Tortoise by Gerald McDermott

Junie B. Jones (series) by Barbara Parks

Lon Po Po by Ed Young

Lord of the Cranes by Kersten Chen

Marvin Redpost (series) by Louis Sacher

Math Curse by Jon Scieszka

Mufaro's Beautiful Daughters by John Steptoe

My Great Aunt Arizona by Gloria Houston

On One Flower: Butterflies, Ticks and a Few More Icks by Anthony D. Fredericks

The Pain and the Great One by Judy Blume

Prince Cinders by Babette Cole

The Recess Queen by Alexis O'Neill

A River Ran Wild by Lynne Cherry

Roll of Thunder, Hear My Cry by Mildred Taylor

The Rough-Face Girl by Rafe Martin

Ruby by Michael Emberley

Sadako by Eleanor Coerr

The Salamander Room by Anne Mazer

Sarah, Plain and Tall by Patricia MacLachlan

Seven Brave Women by Betsy Hearne

Smoky Night by Eve Bunting

So Far from the Sea by Eve Bunting

The Stinky Cheese Man and Other Fairy Stupid Tales by Jon Scieszka

The Summer My Father Was Ten by Pat Brisson

The Talking Eggs by Robert San Souci

Tar Beach by Faith Ringgold

The Teacher from the Black Lagoon by Mike Thaler

The Three Billy Goats Gruff by Paul Galdone

The Three Little Javelinas by Susan Lowell

Thunder Cake by Patricia Polacco

The True Confessions of Charlotte Doyle by Avi

The True Story of the Three Little Pigs by Jon Scieszka

Tuck Everlasting by Natalie Babbitt

Under One Rock: Bugs, Slugs and Other Ughs by Anthony D. Fredericks

The Wednesday Surprise by Eve Bunting

STUDENT-CREATED SCRIPTS

One procedure that will provide students with unique opportunities to practice and master fluency is to give them the chance to design and develop their own scripts. These creations can be done as part of regular writing workshop activities or be easily integrated into extensions of the reading program.

Self-created readers theatre scripts are naturally motivating for students. They provide insights into character development, plot, theme, and setting. Students who are provided with opportunities to create their own scripts (either original scripts or those based on their reading materials) will be actively engaged in the dynamics of a coordinated reading and writing program. Equally important, they will be able to enhance their fluency development in meaningful ways.

The suggestions offered above (for teacher-designed scripts) are also appropriate for students. In addition, you may wish to consider some of the following.

Preparation

Children should be encouraged to work together to design their readers theatre scripts. Small groups of three to four children allow for a multiplicity of options and suggestions for scripting a familiar story. It is advantageous to appoint one youngster within each group to serve as the "Scribe" or "Recorder." Each Recorder should understand that writing goes through many stages, so the first couple of ideas are just that: initial ones, which can be eliminated or expanded according to the wishes and desires of the group.

Writing

Have each group's Recorder write the names of all the identified characters down the left side of a large sheet of poster paper. Other members of a group may suggest possible dialogue for each of the characters as well as the narrator. Movements and actions may also be suggested by group members. I have found it advantageous to consider any props, stage directions, and "set up" after the initial draft of the script. In this way, children can concentrate on the creative expression of their ideas without worrying about some of the minor aspects of their script, all of which can be added later.

Practice

Provide student groups with opportunities to "try out" their drafts on other groups of children. They should watch for the flow of the story, the pace, appropriate dialogue, and, of course, the humor of their script. Just as a playwright will go through many drafts of a play, children should also realize that they may need time to work out the kinks in their productions. By trying out their various drafts on other children, they will have an opportunity to structure and restructure their readers theatre script for maximum impact.

Lesson Plan on Writing Readers Theatre Scripts

You may decide to introduce students to the art of writing readers theatre scripts through one or more formal lesson plans. In this instructional sequence you will model for students the various steps necessary for creating a readers theatre script from a selected book or story (in the basal reader, for example). By going through a step-by-step process, students will gain the confidence necessary to craft their own renditions of popular literature or self-selected stories.

The following lesson plan uses the first few pages of the children's book *The Tsunami Quilt: Grandfather's Story* by Anthony D. Fredericks (reproduced on page 105).

The Tsunami Quilt: Grandfather's Story
by Anthony D. Fredericks
(Chelsea, MI: Sleeping Bear Press, 2007)

When I was little, my grandfather and I went everywhere, always sharing stories and discovering new places. We were the best of friends.

Each year in the spring, Grandmother would make a beautiful lei of plumeria blossoms. She would give it to Grandfather, placing it gently around his neck. Afterwards he and I would drive to Laupāhoehoe Point. He'd ease his old car down the twisting road to the peninsula and park in the grass near the small cove. Then Grandfather and I would walk along the ocean's edge. We would hold hands and watch the sun dance across the waves.

We never talked much on this yearly visit. Somehow I knew it was a time and place for quiet thoughts.

Grandfather always stopped at the marble monument beside the ocean. He would let go of my hand and slowly walk up the stone steps. He would take the lei from around his neck and place it on top of the monument. In silence, he would rest a weathered hand on the stone and stare out over the waves. He would stand there for a long time watching the surf roll in.

Excerpted from *The Tsunami Quilt: Grandfather's Story* © 2007 by Anthony D. Fredericks. Used by permission of the author.

Lesson Plan

Objective:

1. Students will draft a readers theatre script.

Resources:

- *The Tsunami Quilt: Grandfather's Story* by Anthony D. Fredericks

- Overhead projector

- Overhead transparencies

- Transparency pens (various colors)

- Large sheet of newsprint

Procedures:

1. Motivational opening: Read *The Tsunami Quilt* to the class. Stop every so often and invite students to make predictions about the story ("What will happen next?"). Tell students that you will be showing them how to craft a readers theatre script from a children's book using *The Tsunami Quilt* as an example.

2.   Sequential steps:

a)   Place a prepared transparency of the first part of the story on the overhead projector.

b)   Tell students that the first part of the story is known as narration, or the part that tells what is happening in the story.

c)   Mark a section of the text as "Narration" with a blue transparency pen (for example: from "When I was little" to "the surf roll in."

d)   Tell students that this is a section that can be dictated by a narrator, two narrators, a narrator and the main character (Kimo), or some other combination.

e)   Select another transparency—one that includes dialogue—and place it on the overhead projector.

f)   Tell students that this part of the story is known as dialogue, or the part that the characters say.

g)   Mark a section of the text as "Dialogue" with a green transparency pen.

h)   Tell students that this is a section that should be dictated by a specified character (e.g., Grandfather, Kimo, Kimo's father).

i)   Show different sections of the story (via separate transparencies) to the students. Invite students to identify narration sections and dialogue sections. Mark the identified sections with either a blue (narration) or green (dialogue) transparency pen.

j)   Post a sheet of newsprint on a wall. Begin to build the script using a green pen for lines to be said by characters and a blue pen for lines to be said by a narrator. Point out that to maintain audience interest, you may need to modify some lines—typically by shortening them. Also note how you eliminate phrases such as "I pleaded." When you have completed a draft of the script, read it out loud for students. Do a "think aloud" about any revisions or modifications you may need to make in subsequent drafts.

Following is a partial script that might result from the demonstration above:

KIMO: When I was little, my grandfather and I went everywhere. We shared lots of stories and discovered new places.

NARRATOR: Each year in the spring Kimo's grandmother would make a lei from plumeria blossoms and put it around Grandfather's neck.

KIMO: Afterward, Grandfather and I would drive down to Laupāhoehoe Point and park in the grass near the small cove.

GRANDFATHER: Kimo and I would walk along the ocean's edge holding hands and watching the sun dance across the waves.

KIMO: We never talked much on this yearly visit. Somehow I knew it was a time and place for quiet thoughts.

> **NARRATOR:** Kimo's grandfather always stopped at the marble monument and walked up the steps.
>
> **KIMO:** He would take the lei from around his neck and place it on top of the monument.
>
> **NARRATOR:** In silence, he would stand there for a long time and watch the surf roll in.
>
> 3. Conclusion: After students have had an opportunity to review your initial draft of the script, invite them to write (in small groups) the next page of the script. Record their version(s) on individual sheets of newsprint, suggesting any minor editing as necessary. Continue through the remainder of the book until each script is finished. Lead each group in a read-aloud of its initial draft of the script and provide any additional editing as necessary.
>
> **Assessment/Evaluation:**
>
> Invite each group to complete a "Group Self-Report" (see page 108). Take time for each group to summarize its experiences for the class. Collect the forms and review them. Look for areas to emphasize the next time you have the class draft their own readers theatre scripts.

WORKING WITH PARTIAL SCRIPTS

One technique I have found to be extremely useful in helping students design their own readers theatre scripts is to provide them with partial scripts—that is, a script that has been initiated but not completed. I draft the beginning of a script with the necessary characters and some initial dialogue. Then I turn the partial script over to a group of students and invite them to complete the script using their own dialogue or dialogue taken directly from an original source. The group is then charged with the responsibility of finalizing the script and bringing it to a satisfactory conclusion.

On pages 109–10 is a partial script taken from the teacher resource book *Tadpole Tales and Other Totally Terrific Treats for Readers Theatre* by Anthony D. Fredericks. There are some suggested conclusions for students to consider to complete this script.

Whether you use published collections of readers theatre scripts, scripts from the Internet, scripts you create yourself, or scripts developed by your students, you certainly have a wealth of instructional opportunities at your disposal. Most important, you will be able to provide your students with a wide variety of readers theatre opportunities that will reinforce and stimulate their fluency development in very positive ways.

Group Self-Report

Date: _____

Group Members:

_____   _____

_____   _____

_____   _____

Title of Readers Theatre Script:_____

_____

Here is what we included in our script:

_____

_____

_____

_____

Here are some things we thought were challenging:

_____

_____

_____

_____

Here is some additional information or assistance we need:

_____

_____

_____

_____

This is what we like most about our script:

_____

_____

_____

_____

Signed:

_____   _____

_____   _____

_____   _____

Old King Cole Was a Merry Old Soul Until He Had to Do His Math Homework

STAGING: The narrator may be standing off to one side. the other characters may be seated on stools or walking around the staging area.

```
                    Old King Cole
                         X                  Teacher Teacher
                                                  X

    Mandy           Candy            Sandy
      X       X       X                                     Narrator
                                                               X
```

NARRATOR: Old King Cole was a merry old soul. And a merry old soul was he. That is, until he had to do his math homework.

OLD KING COLE: Hey, Teacher Teacher, how come I have to do math homework? I'm a king, you know.

TEACHER TEACHER: Yes, I know, Cole. But you haven't learned how to subtract one number from another. How are you ever going to run a kingdom if you don't know how to subtract?

OLD KING COLE: [pleading] Awwwww, come on, Teacher Teacher. I can hire a bunch of subtracters to do all that work for me. Why should I have to know that stuff?

TEACHER TEACHER: Because you never know when you're going to need it. What will you do when you're not king anymore? You won't be able to hire anybody then.

MANDY: Yeah, king buddy, if someone takes over your kingdom and throws you out, you'll be on your own.

CANDY: Besides, the new king will probably hire all of the subtracters in the land, and there won't be any left for you.

SANDY: That means that you'll have to do all of your subtracting by yourself—with nobody to help you.

TEACHER TEACHER: So, you see, if you don't do your math homework now, you'll never be able to retire.

OLD KING COLE: Dang. There must be something I can do. I just hate math.

Possible Conclusions

1. Old King Cole hires all the kids in the class. He pays them a lot of money to do his math homework for him.

2. Old King Cole buys a computer. He never has to worry about doing math homework again.

3. Old King Cole passes a law making math homework illegal.

4. Old King Cole practices and practices. Soon he becomes the best math student in the entire kingdom.

5. Your idea.

Source: *Tadpole Tales and Other Totally Terrific Treats for Readers Theatre* by Anthony D. Fredericks (Westport, CT: Teacher Ideas Press, 1997), 112–114. Used by permission of the author.

CHAPTER 8

Performing Readers Theatre for an Audience

One of the features of readers theatre I enjoy very much is the many ways in which it can become part of the classroom curriculum. Along with scores of other teachers, I've discovered that readers theatre can be a wonderful way for students to become active participants in the entire learning process as well as a delightful exploration of every curricular area (see chapter 9).

Obviously readers theatre achieves its greatest potency when students have multiple opportunities to share it with others. This chapter focuses on ways you can make that experience incredibly successful.

INITIATING THE PROCESS

You've already seen how readers theatre can become a viable element of your overall reading program in addition to becoming a positive method of enhancing fluency development for all your students. In many ways, it provides youngsters with authentic opportunities to become actively engaged in text.

Script Preparation

One of the advantages of using readers theatre in the classroom or library is the lack of extra work or preparation time necessary to get "up and running." If you use the scripts in this book, your preparation time will be minimal.

❖ After a script has been selected for presentation, make sufficient copies. A copy of the script should be provided for each actor. In addition, making two or three extra copies (one for you and "replacement" copies for scripts that are accidentally damaged or lost) is also a good idea. Copies for the audience are unnecessary and are not suggested.

❖ Bind each script between two sheets of colored construction paper or poster board. Bound scripts tend to formalize the presentation a little and lend an air of professionalism to the actors.

❖ Highlight each character's speaking parts with different color highlighter pens. This helps youngsters track their parts without being distracted by the dialogue of others.

Starting Out

Introducing the concept of readers theatre to students for the first time may be as simple as sharing a script with an entire class and "walking" youngsters through the design and delivery of that script.

❖ Emphasize that a readers theatre performance does not require any memorization of the script. The interpretation and performance are whatcount.

❖ Read an entire script aloud, taking on the various roles. Let students know how easy and comfortable this process is.

❖ Encourage selected volunteers to read assigned parts of a sample script to the entire class. Readers should stand or sit in a circle so that other classmates can observe them.

❖ Provide opportunities for additional re-readings using other volunteers. Plan time to discuss the ease of presentation and the different interpretations offered by various readers.

❖ Allow readers an opportunity to practice their script before presenting it to an audience. Take some time to discuss voice intonation, facial gestures, body movements, and other features that could be used to enhance the presentation.

❖ Give children the opportunity to suggest their own modifications, adaptations, or interpretations of the script. They will undoubtedly be "in tune" with the interests and perceptions of their peers and can offer some distinctive and personal interpretations.

❖ Encourage students to select nonstereotypical roles within any readers theatre script. For example, boys may take on female roles and girls may take on male roles, the smallest person in the class may take on the role of a giant fire-breathing dragon (for example), or a shy student may take on the role of a boastful, bragging giant. Provide sufficient opportunities for students to expand and extend their appreciation of readers theatre through a variety of "out of character" roles.

Staging

Staging involves the physical location of the readers as well as any necessary movements. Unlike a more formal play, the movements are often minimal. The emphasis is more on presentation, less on action.

❖ For most presentations, readers will stand or sit on stools or chairs. The physical location of each reader has been indicated for each of the scripts in this book.

❖ If there are many characters in the presentation, it may be advantageous to have characters in the rear (upstage) standing while those in the front (downstage) are seated on stools or chairs. This ensures that the audience will both see and hear every actor.

❖ Usually all of the characters will be on stage throughout the duration of the presentation. For most presentations it is not necessary to have characters enter and exit. If you seat the characters on stools, they may face the audience when they are involved in a particular scene and then turn around whenever they are not involved in a scene.

❖ Make simple hand-lettered signs with the name of each character. Loop a piece of string or yarn through each sign and hang it around the neck of each respective character. That way, the audience will know the identity of each character throughout the presentation.

❖ Each reader will have her or his own copy of the script in a paper cover (see above). If possible, use a music stand for each reader's script (this allows readers to use their hands for dramatic interpretations as necessary).

❖ Several presentations have a narrator to set up the story. The narrator serves to establish the place and time of the story for the audience so that the characters can "jump into" their parts from the beginning. Typically, the narrator is separated from the other "actors" and can be identified by a simple sign.

Props

Two positive features of readers theatre are its ease of preparation and its ease of presentation. Informality is a hallmark of any readers theatre script.

❖ Much of the setting for a story should take place in the audience's mind. Elaborate scenery is not necessary; simple props are often the best. For example:

   – A branch or potted plant may serve as a tree.

   – A drawing on the chalkboard may illustrate a building.

   – A hand-lettered sign may designate one part of the staging area as a particular scene (e.g., swamp, castle, field, forest).

   – Children's toys may be used for uncomplicated props (e.g., telephone, vehicles, etc.).

   – A sheet of aluminum foil or a remnant of blue cloth may be used to simulate a lake or pond.

❖ Costumes for the actors are unnecessary. A few simple items may be suggested by students. For example:

   – Hats, scarves, or aprons may be used by major characters.

   – A paper cutout may serve as a tie, button, or badge.

   – Old clothing (borrowed from parents) may be used as warranted.

❖ Some teachers and librarians have discovered that the addition of appropriate background music or sound effects enhances a readers theatre presentation.

❖ It's important to remember that the emphasis in readers theatre is on the reading, not on any accompanying "features." The best presentations are often the simplest.

Delivery

I've often found it useful to let students know that the only difference between a readers theatre presentation and a movie role is that they will have a script in their hands. This allows them to focus more on presenting a script rather than on memorizing it.

❖ When first introduced to readers theatre, students often have a tendency to "read into" their scripts. Encourage students to look up from their scripts and interact with other characters or the audience as appropriate.

❖ Practicing the script beforehand can eliminate the problem of students burying their heads in the pages. Children will understand the need to involve the audience as much as possible in the development of the story.

❖ Voice projection and delivery are important in allowing the audience to understand character actions. The proper mood and intent need to be established, which is possible when children are familiar and comfortable with each character's "style."

❖ Again, the emphasis is on delivery, so be sure to suggest different types of voice (i.e., angry, irritated, calm, frustrated, excited, etc.) that children may wish to use for their particular character(s).

Post-Presentation

As a wise author once said, "The play's the thing." So it is with readers theatre. In other words, the mere act of presenting a readers theatre script is complete in and of itself. It is not necessary, or even required, to do any type of formalized evaluation after readers theatre. Once again, the emphasis is on informality. Readers theatre should and can be a pleasurable and stimulating experience for children.

Following are a few ideas you may want to share with students. In doing so, you will be providing youngsters with important learning opportunities that extend and promote all aspects of your reading and language arts program.

❖ After a presentation, discuss with students how the script enhanced or altered the original story.

❖ Invite students to suggest other characters who could be added to the script.

❖ Invite students to suggest alternate dialogue for various characters.

❖ Invite students to suggest different setting(s) for the script.

❖ Invite students to talk about their reactions to various characters' expressions, tone of voice, presentations, or dialogues.

❖ After a presentation, invite youngsters to suggest modifications they think could be made to the script.

"IT'S SHOW TIME!"

After scripts have been prepared or selected by you and your students, it's time to consider how, when, and where you would like to present them. There are many options to consider. The following list, which is not all-inclusive, includes a variety of presentation options for readers theatre. How you and your students present readers theatre will ultimately be determined by the nature of your overall reading program, the time and facilities available, the comfort level of students, and the demands of your curriculum. Suffice it to say that there is an almost inexhaustible array of options available.

Suggested Presentation Options for Readers Theatre

❖ One group of students presents a script to another group.

❖ One group of students presents to the entire class.

❖ Several groups of students present to the entire class (an in-class "readers theatre festival").

❖ One group of students presents to another class at the same grade level.

❖ Several groups of students present to another class at the same grade level.

❖ One group of students presents to a class at a higher or lower grade level.

❖ Several groups of students present to a class at a higher or lower grade level.

❖ One group of students presents to the entire school (at an all-school assembly).

❖ Several groups of students present to the entire school (at an all-school assembly).

❖ One group of students in the class presents to an audience of parents, school personnel, the school principal, and other interested individuals.

❖ Several groups of students in the class present to an audience of parents, school personnel, the school principal, and other interested individuals.

❖ One group of students produces a readers theatre script that is videotaped and distributed throughout the school and/or district.

❖ Several groups of students produce a readers theatre script that is videotaped and distributed throughout the school and/or district.

❖ Students join with students from another class to co-present readers theatre scripts at a grade level or an all-school literacy celebration.

It is important to share some of these options with your students and invite them to identify those with which they would be most comfortable. My rule of thumb is to "start small" at first—for example, have one or two groups of students present to the class as part of a regularly scheduled readers theatre presentation time (once a month, for example). As students gain confidence and self-assurance, they should be encouraged to take their presentations "on the road," sharing them with other classes and other grades.

It is also important to remember that there is no single way to present readers theatre. What follows are some ideas you and the youngsters with whom you work may wish to keep in mind as you put on the productions in this book, productions from another readers theatre book, those you have created based on popular children's literature, or scripts generated by students as part of their reading and writing experiences. These considerations are appropriate whether readers theatre is shared in a classroom setting or the school library.

Script Selection

One of the best presentation options is when several groups of students in your classroom come together to present a selection of readers theatre scripts for an audience of enthusiastic students (from the same or a different grade) and some very appreciative parents. Here are some points for you to consider:

❖ When possible, invite students to select a variety of scripts to be included in the presentation. Inform them that a combination of short scripts and longer scripts adds variety to the program. When students are invited to be part of the selection process a sense of "ownership" develops, which contributes to the ultimate success of the overall presentation(s).

❖ Consider the age and grade of the audience. For younger students (grades K–2) the total program should be no longer than 25 minutes (a mix of three to five scripts). For older students (grades 3–6) the total program should be no longer than 45 minutes (a mix of five to seven scripts).

❖ If feasible, include a section of the program (parts of a script or an entire production) in which the audience takes an active role. This could include singing, clapping, repeating selected lines in a production (provide cue cards), or some other physical contribution. This would be particularly appropriate for younger audiences, whose attention span is typically short and sporadic.

❖ Include a mix of several of the following possibilities.

- teacher-created scripts
- student-created scripts
- scripts from familiar books
- scripts from books requiring little or no rewriting (see chapter 7)
- scripts from books requiring some rewriting

Inviting an Audience

As students become more comfortable with readers theatre, they will want to perform for an audience. An audience gives readers theatre legitimacy—it is a signal to students that all their hard work and practice has a purpose: to share the fruits of their labors (and their concomitant improvements in reading fluency) with an appreciative group of individuals.

❖ Consider sending announcements or invitations to parents and other interested individuals. You may wish to design these yourself or, better yet, invite students to design, illustrate, and produce the invitations. Here is one example:

You Are Invited!

Dear Parents:

We would like to invite you to a most exciting event in Miss Smithton's third grade classroom—a readers theatre celebration! Students have been working hard practicing their reading, rehearsing their scripts, and planning this wonderful event.

You'll hear fantastic stories, delightful tales, and incredible literature. Best of all, you'll see some future Hollywood stars (including your child) in action!

Join us for an afternoon of fun and adventure:

Date: Friday, October 28

Where: Room 203 (2nd Floor), Halprin Elementary School

Time: 2:00—2:45 p.m.

Refreshments will be served after the presentations.

Sincerely,

Roberta Smithton

❖ In addition to parents, I have always found it appropriate (and exciting) to invite other adults with whom the students are familiar, including the school secretary, the custodian, a bus driver or two, cafeteria workers, and aides, for example. After the presentation the students are sure to get a raft of positive comments and lots of appreciation from these individuals as they encounter them throughout the school.

❖ As appropriate, invite community members to be part of the audience. Residents of a local senior citizen center or retirement home are a most logical (and very enthusiastic) audience. These folks are always appreciative of the work of children and are often eager to see what is happening in the local schools.

Program

Work with students to assemble a program that outlines the various scripts and presentations that will be taking place on the target day. A program formalizes the entire production and also serves as a wonderful souvenir for students long after the day is over.

Following is a sample program.

Mrs. Paulboro's Pirates
present

An Afternoon of Readers Theatre
Friday, March 24, 2006

1. *Amazing Grace* by Mary Hoffman
   Actors: Maria, Nicole, Brian, Taylor, Celia

2. Selected poems from *Joyful Noise* by Paul Fleischman
   Actors: Ernesto, Grady, Brice

3. *Bringing the Rain to Kapiti Plain* by Verna Aardema
   Actors: Nance, Karen, Nic

4. *My Wonderful Grandmother Bernice*—an adaptation of *My Great-Aunt Arizona* by Gloria Houston
   Authored by: Candice and Alicia
   Actors: Candice, Alicia, Stephanie, Peggy

5. A rendition of *'Twas the Night* by Jon Scieszka (based on The Night Before Christmas)
   Actors: Tyrone, Marshall, Bruce, Tian

6. *The Attack of the Math Monster* (an original story)
   Authored by: Carol, De'Shaun, Pedro
   Actors: Carol, De'Shaun, Pedro

❖ You may want to provide each student with a copy of the program (in an inexpensive cardboard frame) that has been autographed by each of the performers.

❖ Consider working with the art teacher or a graphic artist to design a special program that is both colorful and stylistic.

Presenting readers theatre scripts can be as elaborate or extensive as you wish. You will discover, as I have, that the degree of formality you want to inject into readers theatre will be determined by the productions you wish to present, the inclinations of your students, and the opportunities available in your classroom schedule.

As children become more familiar with and polished in using readers theatre, they will be able to suggest a multitude of presentation possibilities for future scripts. It is important to help children assume a measure of self-initiated responsibility in the delivery of any readers theatre. In so doing, you will be helping to ensure their personal engagement and active participation in this most valuable of language arts activities.

CHAPTER 9

Using Readers Theatre to Develop Fluency Across the Curriculum

Readers theatre has proven itself as a viable element in the classroom reading program. But its utility isn't restricted to just reading—it provides you with many more teaching opportunities, and your students with an abundance of learning opportunities, across the curriculum. The utility of readers theatre as an instructional tool allows you to capitalize on its advantages and benefits (see chapter 4) in almost every subject area.

As you begin integrating readers theatre into your classroom curriculum, you will be underscoring the value of reading as a learning tool in every subject. Often youngsters (particularly those who are struggling readers) have the perception that reading is only a "subject" that takes place between 9:00 and 10:30 every morning, for example, or see it as an activity that is pursued only with a basal text. As a result, too many youngsters get the idea that reading is regulated by the clock or by an obscure publisher in a distant city. Reading is frequently viewed as a classroom-based subject rather than as a vehicle for learning.

However, when reading instruction is integrated into all aspects of the elementary curriculum, students' literacy growth and development mushrooms exponentially. One of the distinct advantages of readers theatre is that it allows you to incorporate readers theatre as a viable element in every curricular area. You can promote and support students' fluency development far beyond the reading curriculum. Reading fluency can be an important and integral part of every subject you teach—particularly when it is promoted through readers theatre.

TWO CLASSROOMS

Fifth Grade

Matt Bowman has been teaching fifth grade for 10 years. Originally from San Francisco, he now resides just outside Denver, Colorado. His classroom is a delightful mix of cultures, languages, and abilities. Or, as Matt says, "I've got the entire United Nations in one room!"

With so many levels and abilities in his classroom, teaching reading has always been a challenge for Matt. He has worked hard to provide his students with appropriate reading opportunities. Several years ago, Matt attended a readers theatre presentation by the author of this book. He was instantly taken by the possibilities for incorporating readers theatre into his overall reading program. But he also saw the benefits that might accrue when readers theatre was made part of the other subjects he taught.

Matt began to develop some readers theatre scripts for selected parts of his social studies curriculum. He also obtained teacher resource books of prepared scripts to use with his students. Slowly he began to integrate selected scripts into his overall program. The level of enthusiasm and interest displayed by his students indicated that they wanted more! As one of his students so aptly put it, "This readers theatre stuff really makes social studies interesting, not like the stuff in our textbook!"

One of the themes Matt shares every year revolves around the Civil War. As part of a complete unit, Matt provides his students with a script from the teacher resource book *Readers Theatre for American History* by Anthony D. Fredericks. The first few sections of that script are presented on page 121.

Matt quickly discovered that readers theatre brought social studies alive for his students. Students were actively engaged in the dynamics of history and began to see it as much more than a simple recording of facts. They began to understand that history is the story of people and events.

Matt also saw impressive improvements in students' fluency development. They were able to read with higher levels of comprehension as well as increased levels of "literary comfortableness" (Matt's words). Just as important, students began to understand that reading could be a significant learning tool in any subject area.

Second Grade

Myra Weaver has recently completed her first year of teaching second grade in a rural school district east of Tampa, Florida. She was introduced to readers theatre at a conference presentation by this author in Orlando and fell in love with its possibilities. Over the course of the year she used readers theatre as an important component of her classroom reading program. But she has also seen its possibilities in various content areas.

Just after initiating a new science unit on weathering and erosion, Myra provides her students with a readers theatre script from the book *Nonfiction Readers Theatre for Beginning Readers* (Fredericks 2007). The script is used as part of her reading lessons on fluency and comprehension development, but also serves as a way for students to "get into" the dynamics of weathering and erosion in an active way. As Myra says, "I saw this script as a wonderful way to address two of my most important goals for these kids: fluency development and inquiry-based science. I wanted the kids to see the role of reading in science and how reading can help us enjoy science more."

The first few sections of that script are presented on page 122.

One Day in Gettysburg

JEB: Good day to you all.

ALL: Good day, Jeb.

BETH: Good day, everyone. Is everyone here for the president's speech?

JOHN: Yes. I wonder what he's going to talk about?

SAMUEL: I don't know. But I do know this: Ever since those first shots were fired at Fort Sumter back in April of 1861, there sure has been a lot of blood spilled.

HANNA: And all those boys—those young boys—who lost their lives. My sister's boy was among them; bright kid, not more than 16 years old. He would have made a good farmer, too. But he was given a gun and some ammunition, and, well, I guess you know the rest . . . [trails off]

JEB: It's a darn shame. Shot and killed, thousands of them, just shot and killed. Bodies lying all over the fields. That battle at Bull Run in July of 1861 started it all. The Union thought the battle would end the war. They never expected the South to be so strong. That was a tough defeat. I guess people figured that the war was going to be a lot longer than they expected.

HANNA: Hey, let's listen . . . the president's about to speak.

PRESIDENT LINCOLN: [mightily and powerfully] "Four score and seven years ago our fathers brought forth, upon this continent, a new nation, conceived in Liberty, and dedicated to the proposition that all men are created equal."

SAMUEL: I'll say one thing, Mr. Lincoln sure does know how to start a speech. It makes me feel good that he helps us remember where we came from, you know, where our country began.

Excerpted from *Readers Theatre for American History* by Anthony D. Fredericks (Westport, CT: Teacher Ideas Press, 2001), pg. 71-77. Used by permission of the author.

Let's Rock and Roll!

SCIENTIST 1: You know, I was just thinking about the planet Earth.

SCIENTIST 2: Why were you thinking about Earth?

SCIENTIST 1: Well, I think Earth is a pretty amazing place to live.

SCIENTIST 2: You're right, there.

SCIENTIST 1: It's amazing for many reasons. There is something cool about the earth.

SCIENTIST 2: What's that?

SCIENTIST 1: Earth is always changing. Something is always happening to the earth.

SCIENTIST 2: You're right. Some of the changes take a long time. Some changes don't take much time at all.

SCIENTIST 1: The slow changes are some of the most interesting. Those are changes that take a long, l-l-l-o-o-o-n-n-n-g-g-g time. Like when the Grand Canyon was made.

SCIENTIST 2: What did you have in mind?

SCIENTIST 1: Well, "weathering," for one.

SCIENTIST 2: Yeah, I know what "weathering" is. Weathering is when rock is broken down at the earth's surface.

SCIENTIST 1: That happens all the time. Water flows into the cracks of a large rock. Sometimes the water freezes. When water freezes, it expands. So when water in the crack of a rock freezes it, too, expands. Then the rock breaks apart.

Excerpted from *Nonfiction Readers Theatre for Beginning Readers* by Anthony D. Fredericks (Westport, CT: Teacher Ideas Press, 2007). Used by permission of the author.

 From *Building Fluency with Readers Theatre: Motivational Strategies, Successful Lessons and Dynamic Scripts to Develop Fluency, Comprehension, Writing, and Vocabulary* by Anthony D. Fredericks. Westport, CT: Teacher Ideas Press. Copyright © 2008.

As Myra stated, "Here was a wonderful opportunity for my students to see how reading and science go together. But, it was also an opportunity for me to use readers theatre to enhance their fluency development in a new way."

Since making readers theatre a regular part of her science lessons, Myra has seen dramatic improvements in students' fluency growth and development. She also has another vehicle for integrating reading across the content areas in addition to helping students use their reading skills in meaningful ways. Myra is enthusiastic about readers theatre. "It's one of the most exciting things I've shared with students this year. It really gives me a powerful new teaching tool to extend reading into every subject."

USING READERS THEATRE IN THE CONTENT AREAS

We know that students in reading-rich classrooms demonstrate increased levels of comprehension as well as strong reading interests. The overall literacy growth of students who are provided with learning opportunities in which reading is woven into and throughout all learning tasks is multiplied exponentially. Students can reap enormous literary benefits when they are surrounded by positive reading experiences and provided with activities that have intrinsic motivation for them.

What I am suggesting is that students (of all levels and all abilities) can profit enormously when reading is integrated into all aspects of the elementary curriculum. An integrated curriculum has magnificent possibilities for readers of every stripe and inclination. By integrating reading into all curricular areas, you are helping youngsters understand that reading just doesn't occur during a specific time of the day (9:00–10:30) or with specific kinds of books (e.g., textbooks). By designing activities and experiences in which reading and literature are inherent parts of every curricular area, you are assisting children in understanding the role reading has in all our lives—whether young or old. A broad-based reading program—one that includes all the language arts in all the content areas—underscores the value of reading as both a tool for learning and a way to comprehend any educational task.

The value of readers theatre has been well documented throughout this book. That it can positively influence literacy growth in a wide variety of areas has been sufficiently emphasized. Just as important, readers theatre is an effective research-based approach that integrates reading into each and every content area. Whenever you want to emphasize the value (and roles) of speaking, writing, listening, and reading in any content area, readers theatre provides a positive vehicle to make that happen. In short, when readers theatre is made part of any subject area, the possibilities for active involvement, positive learning, and increased comprehension are magnified enormously.

Figure 9.1 (pp. 124–27) provides a wide range of possibilities for including readers theatre in your language arts, science, social studies, math, music, and art programs. Use these as possibilities for your own classroom. You may wish to work with your colleagues to develop other possibilities for your grade level or individual classroom program. By integrating readers theatre into your instructional program, you will discover incredible opportunities to promote fluency far beyond the objectives and standards of your reading curriculum.

Figure 9.1. Extending the Elementary Curriculum with Readers Theatre

Language Arts

General Extensions

- To initiate an author study, invite students to perform and participate in a readers theatre adaptation of one of the author's books. Students may also wish to create their own readers theatre production from the author's life or another one of his or her books as a culminating activity.
- After students have participated in a literature circle, ask them to select a favorite scene and develop it into a readers theatre script.
- Most basal textbooks in language arts and reading are thematically based. Introduce each theme with a readers theatre script based on a literature selection related to the theme or profiled in the unit.
- Invite students to create their own readers theatre scripts as part of your regular writing workshop activities.
- Students may enjoy participating in a selection of readers theatre scripts from the teacher resource book *Mother Goose Readers Theatre for Beginning Readers* by Anthony D. Fredericks. These scripts can be used as part of a Mother Goose unit—either to introduce the unit or as a series of culminating activities.

Book-Specific Extensions

- To initiate a unit on international folktales, or folktales in general, invite students to participate in one or more readers theatre scripts created from several of Gerald McDermott's books, such as *How Raven Got the Sun*, *Zomo the Rabbit*, and *Jabuti the Tortoise.*
- Develop *Brown Bear, Brown Bear, What Do You See?* by Bill Martin Jr. into a readers theatre script to help your beginning readers focus on the phonemic awareness skill of rhyming and alliteration.
- *Bringing the Rain to Kapiti Plain* by Verna Aardema can be developed into a readers theatre script as part of a unit on poetry, particularly narrative poetry or international poetry.
- Invite select groups of students to each create a readers theatre script based on a favorite scene from Avi's *The True Confessions of Charlotte Doyle*. Each script could focus on a particular personality trait of the main character—either during the story or as a possible sequel (Charlotte's life several years later).
- As part of a study on biographies, invite students to create their own readers theatre version of Doreen Rappaport's *Martin's Big Words* or Nikki Giovanni's *Rosa*.

Science

General Extensions

- To initiate a new unit, start with a readers theatre script—created by you or selected from a collection of readers theatre scripts. Students will be more excited about a forthcoming unit when asked to participate in a related script.
- Instead of having students write a research report about what they learned in a specific unit, ask them to develop (perhaps in small groups) their own readers theatre scripts about selected topics in that unit. These scripts can be presented to other classes.
- Instead of the traditional science fair, invite students to create a readers theatre fair in which select groups (or entire classes) create and present readers theatre presentations about specific scientific concepts and principles.

- Use part of a readers theatre script as the motivational opening or anticipatory set for a new lesson. After students have completed the lesson, ask them to present the second half of the script as part of the lesson conclusion or summary.
- The life of a specific scientist may be presented through a readers theatre script. Readers theatre provides students with unique opportunities to "walk in the shoes" of another person and bring life to that person's story. It can eliminate the stereotypical views that people often have of scientists (e.g., frizzy hair, lab coats, glasses, pocket protectors, etc.).

Book-Specific Extensions

- After students have finished reading *The Dinosaurs of Waterhouse Hawkins* by Barbara Kerley, invite them to create a readers theatre script about the life of the central character.
- Introduce the various dimensions, sizes, and measurement of selected animals via a readers theatre script and then invite students to read *Actual Size* by Steve Jenkins. Afterward, students may participate in various measuring activities using family pets or information gathered from other books.
- A script based on one or more of the poems in *Song of the Water Boatman and Other Pond Poems* by Joyce Sidman may be used to introduce children to life in an aquatic ecosystem.
- Students will thoroughly enjoy developing one or more of Jon Scieszka's poems in *Science Verse* into a mini-readers theatre script. Each script may be presented in advance of a unit of study represented by each poem (e.g., water cycle, dinosaurs, food chains, states of matter).
- As part of a culminating project for a study of leaves, invite students to participate in a readers theatre script using Lois Ehlert's *Leaf Man*. This delightful tale is filled with numerous possibilities for readers theatre.
- *The Tsunami Quilt: Grandfather's Story* by Anthony D. Fredericks can be developed into a reader theatre script and presented to students as part of a unit on natural disasters—particularly the impact of natural disasters on human life.

Social Studies

General Extensions

- Working in concert with the school librarian (see below), plan a unit that takes advantage of social studies books and resources in the library as well as books and resources in your classroom. Both library and classroom time can be used for the creation, practice, and performance of social studies–related readers theatre scripts.
- Challenge students to create a readers theatre script that summarizes the major concepts in a chapter in your social studies textbook. Students can present their production to another class (at your grade level) as a way of introducing them to that particular subject.
- Use several of the prepared scripts in *Readers Theatre for American History* by Anthony D. Fredericks as introductions to select topics in American history. After students have performed a script, invite them to discuss its implications in the context of the information presented in the textbook.
- Invite students to work in pairs or triads to create biographical readers theatre scripts about selected historical figures. Keep these on file to use in succeeding years while also inviting future classes to create additional biographical scripts.

Figure 9.1. Extending the Elementary Curriculum with Readers Theatre (*Continued*)

- Invite students to create a readers theatre script that changes a historical event or alters a part of history. For example, invite them to draft a script in which Lincoln survives his attempted assassination. Or what about a script in which the west coast was settled first and there was an "eastward movement" across the country? Or perhaps a script in which women were never given the right to vote. Plan sufficient time for students to discuss the implications of their historical "rewritings."

Book-Specific Extensions

- A scene from Eve Bunting's *So Far from the Sea* may be used to set the stage for a discussion of the Japanese internment camps set up during World War II.
- After students have read Gloria Huston's *My Great-Aunt Arizona*, invite them to participate in a readers theatre adaptation of the book. The script could be based on teaching in a rural environment or life in Appalachia.
- Students may wish to create a sequel (in the form of a readers theatre script) for Jaqueline Woodson's *The Other Side*. Students may wish to predict what happens to the fence or to the relationship between the two girls in later years. Such a discussion could be an appropriate activity after a lesson on racial segregation practices.
- Pat Mora's *Tomás and the Library Lady* is an excellent book to develop into a readers theatre script for use in a unit on migrant workers. Spanish-speaking students may wish to create an alternate version in their native language.
- The Oklahoma land rush and the contributions of African Americans during that time period may be illustrated in a teacher-made readers theatre script based on Joyce Carol Thomas's *I Have Heard of a Land*.

Math

General Extensions

- Some mathematical topics are less stimulating than others. When interest wanes, provide students with a chance to "re-energize" by creating a readers theatre script on the topic.
- Instead of the typical end-of-chapter test after a particular mathematical principle (e.g., long division, fractions) has been taught, invite students to create their own readers theatre script that uses five (or eight, or three) of the basic concepts.
- Ask the school librarian to select several mathematics-related books for your students. Ask students to develop an appropriate readers theatre script for each one. Then ask students to perform their presentations for other classes studying those concepts.
- Create a readers theatre script about a famous mathematician. Invite students to perform the script as part of a grade-level "Math Fair."
- Invite students to rewrite a section of the math textbook as a readers theatre script by inserting selected class members into the text. For example: "Tara: If I divide five by two, I'm going to have something left over, aren't I? Sam: Yes, you will. Tara: So, what should I do?"

Book-Specific Extensions

- The concept of division may be shared with students using a teacher-created readers theatre script based on Pat Hutchins's book *The Doorbell Rang*.
- Higher forms of addition may be introduced with a teacher-created adaptation of *Anno's Magic Seeds* by Mitsumasa Anno.

- Counting concepts may be effectively reinforced with a script based on the book *More M&M's Brand Chocolate Candies Math* by Barbara Barbieri McGrath and Roger Glass.
- Simple counting concepts may be taught and supported with a readers theatre script based on the book *Ten Little Rabbits* by Virginia Grossman and Sylvia Long.
- Accuracy in measuring may be reinforced with a teacher-created readers theatre script based on the book *How Long Is It? (Rookie Read-About Math)* by Donna Loughran.

Art and Music

General Extensions

- One way to introduce specific artists or musicians to students would be to involve them in the preparation and presentation of readers theatre scripts about the lives of selected individuals.
- As part of a concluding activity on a style of painting (e.g., impressionism, pointillism), invite students to create a readers theatre production that summarizes essential elements or factual information.
- Invite students to create an original script about how a specific form of music (e.g., folk music, rock and roll) has been influential in American history. The script, of course, would have an appropriate musical accompaniment.
- Invite students to sing a readers theatre script. For example, a rap version about a popular musical artist might be appropriate.
- Students may wish to create a series of readers theatre scripts using a variety of artistic formats (e.g., torn paper collages, calligraphy).
- Students may wish to create, and eventually perform, a script that uses the lyrics from a popular song.

Book-Specific Extensions

- As an introduction to art museums, ask students to participate in a teacher-created readers theatre script based on *Babar's Museum of Art* by Laurent De Brunhoff.
- In advance of a field trip to the art museum, introduce students to a readers theatre script using *Squeaking of Art, the Mice Go to the Museum* by Monica Wellington.
- Introduce students to the lives of famous artists with appropriate literature. For example, a teacher-created readers theatre script based on *Draw with Pablo Picasso* by Ana Salvador would be a great introduction to the world of art.
- Provide students with a unique insight into the lives of musicians by providing readers theatre scripts based on selected groups or individuals. For example, a teacher-created script developed from *The Rolling Stones (Rock & Roll Hall of Famers)* by Thomas Forget (part of a series) would be a wonderful introduction to the people behind the music.
- A scene from *Sebastian: A Book about Bach* by Jeanette Winter may be used to set the stage for a study of famous composers.

TEACHERS AND LIBRARIANS: THE DYNAMIC DUO

Elementary teachers and school librarians have long known intuitively, and it has been validated with a significant body of research, is that the literature shared in both classroom and library has wide-ranging and long-lasting implications for the educational and social development of children. More important, however, is the unassailable fact that when teachers and librarians join together to promote literature collaboratively, they are opening incredible windows that expand the influence of that literature and extend the learning opportunities for youngsters as never before.

In preparation for writing this book, I talked with school librarians and teachers throughout the United States. I discovered that the "collaboration factor" had a significant influence on the ultimate success of readers theatre. A substantial level of cooperation between the classroom teacher and the school librarian was essential if readers theatre were to be made a successful element and a dynamic feature of any language arts curriculum. The partnership between teacher and librarian is, and continues to be, the crucial element in the success children enjoy within and throughout any academic endeavor.

As you might imagine, this partnership does not happen overnight. It involves a mutual sharing of ideas, possibilities, and projects. But when teachers and librarians band together, the curricular effect of readers theatre can be expanded exponentially. It involves trust and coordination, but the overall effect is more than worth the effort.

Benefits

In my discussions with elementary school librarians and classroom teachers, I discovered the following benefits in a collaborative partnership between these individuals:

- Readers theatre projects can be designed, developed, and taught over an extended period of time (days, weeks).

- The Reading/English Language Arts Standards can be promoted in a coordinated and systematic fashion.

- Library programs can be effectively coordinated with classroom programs for both the short and long term.

- More time is available for instructional purposes. A partnership between a teacher and the school librarian can expand the instructional possibilities of readers theatre.

- Language arts is promoted as a continuous activity, rather than a subject taught only in a classroom.

- There is a greater emphasis on language arts as a continuous process of problem solving and critical thinking.

- Language arts can be woven into all aspects of the elementary curriculum. Readers theatre offers instructional possibilities that expand and extend teaching and learning opportunities beyond traditional practices.

- Both literature and readers theatre are promoted as viable and exciting models of literacy in action.

- Cooperative teaching and cooperative learning can be promoted simultaneously.

Forging the Partnership

When teachers and librarians work together, great things happen. When they do so as an essential ingredient of the reading and language arts curriculum, then fantastic things happen! What follows is a list of the ways in which teachers and librarians can develop a partnership that is mutually supportive, educationally sound, and dynamically oriented toward a coordinated approach to readers theatre.

- Teachers and librarians should plan to team teach readers theatre units.

- Teachers should invite the librarian into their classrooms to introduce readers theatre and any accompanying literature.

- Librarians should invite teachers into the library to introduce readers theatre (to their classes) and any accompanying literature.

- Teachers should provide the school librarian with a list of language arts topics and assignments to be tackled throughout the year. Teachers should then work with the librarian to make suggestions regarding available resources—specifically readers theatre.

- Teachers and librarians should develop joint projects in which selected literature is introduced in the library and followed up with specific instructional activities (i.e., readers theatre) in the classroom.

- Teachers and librarians should develop joint projects in which selected literature is introduced in the classroom and followed up with specific instructional activities (i.e., readers theatre) in the library.

- Librarians should introduce students to specific literature selections with appropriate follow-up activities (i.e., readers theatre) for use in the classroom.

- Teachers should introduce students to specific literature selections with appropriate follow-up activities (i.e., readers theatre) for use in the library.

- Invite students to create their own readers theatre scripts after reading selected (and assigned) books in the library.

The possibilities for a coordinated approach to readers theatre—between school librarians and classroom teachers—are astronomical! Students are provided with engaging and lasting learning opportunities, teachers have multiple ways of sharing the vitality of language arts, and librarians can promote literature far beyond the walls of the school library. When teachers and librarians work together, the educational benefits of readers theatre mushroom.

CHAPTER 10

Questions and Answers

I have had the privilege and honor of being invited into many classrooms to witness groups of students performing readers theatre using scripts from some of my published books (see chapter 7). I have also had the delightful opportunity to share my passion for readers theatre in seminars, conferences, and workshops all across the United States and Canada. What I have learned is that readers theatre can be a wonderfully creative addition to any classroom and any reading program. To see the enthusiasm in the eyes of students and witness high levels of participation in an activity that enhances literacy development for all is truly a joy.

As I talk with teachers in my workshops and classroom visits, they often pepper me with a host of questions about readers theatre and its role in enhancing reading fluency. I've collected many of those questions below, along with my responses. As you have read this book, you too, might have had some questions about fluency and the role that readers theatre has in promoting high levels of fluent reading. I hope that some of the more "popular" questions (and answers) recorded below will provide you with the additional data you seek.

"I have a very crowded curriculum. How do I fit readers theatre into my day?"

Incorporating readers theatre into your classroom plans doesn't mean that you have to make major adjustments to your schedule. Readers theatre provides you with some unique instructional opportunities to promote reading, writing, listening, and speaking in all aspects of your curriculum. You will discover a wealth of opportunities to use readers theatre as an adjunct in not only reading, but language arts, social studies, science, and other aspects of the elementary curriculum. In short, readers theatre is not an *addition* to the curriculum, but rather an *enhancement* of the curriculum. It is also a most unique way to build bridges among all the language arts and all the content areas. Most important, however, you will notice heightened levels of excitement and enthusiasm in students as they participate in and create readers theatre scripts.

"What about the standards? Will readers theatre help my students master grade-level standards?"

Readers theatre embraces 11 of the 12 standards for reading and language arts (see pages 58–59). It is one of the few activities available to teachers that addresses so many of the national standards at the same time. Undoubtedly those standards are embedded throughout your basal reading program and are listed in the unit goals in your teacher's manual. As you review a unit prior to teaching it, you will see many opportunities to integrate readers theatre into the dynamics of your instructional plans. From writing to communicating, from research skills to comprehension development, readers theatre offers a host of learning opportunities just as it provides a host of teaching opportunities.

"Is fluency really that important? How come I've never heard of it before?"

Fluency isn't a new concept. It has been part of reading instruction for a long, long time. We may have used different terms and different practices, but fluency has always been part and parcel of reading instruction. In the "good old days" we promoted fluency through a (now discouraged) technique known as "round robin reading." In this practice students (in a small group) would each read a selected piece of a story for the teacher. The teacher would listen carefully for accurate and fluent reading—correcting mistakes and encouraging each student to read in a smooth and rhythmic pattern. Although we no longer advocate that particular instructional practice, we have discovered that fluency plays a major role in each student's reading growth. Throughout this book you have read about many researchers who have provided convincing data about the significance of fluency as well as how readers theatre can enhance, promote, and stimulate readers to "read and comprehend efficiently and with appropriate expression" (Fredericks 2008b).

"Will readers theatre really help my struggling readers?"

Many struggling readers view reading as a very passive activity. They often see lifeless forms (words) on a sheet of paper (book page) that may be difficult to decode and equally difficult to understand. These students often see reading as something that is done to them, rather than something in which they can take an active role. Readers theatre is a way for these readers to engage in a vibrant, dynamic, and active relationship with words, sentences, and stories. Students become manipulators of language, instead of being manipulated by language. They can actively process language for their own benefit—and, as a result, they experience increased levels of motivation, fluency, and comprehension.

"I just don't have the time to write lots of readers theatre scripts for my students. What can I do?"

You don't need to write your own scripts to be able to incorporate readers theatre into your classroom. There are plenty of teacher resource books brimming with collections of readers theatre scripts for every grade level and every ability level. Many of these are listed in chapter 7 of this book. Here you will find humorous scripts, social studies scripts, fairy tale scripts, science scripts, scripts for beginning readers, scripts of folktales and legends, as well as a plethora of scripts that embrace every single area of the elementary curriculum. I have had the privilege of writing more than a dozen readers theatre books for classroom use—and will continue to do so, simply because of the inexhaustible range of subjects and topics that can be enhanced via readers theatre.

"How much time should I devote to readers theatre?"

There is no simple answer here. It will all depend on the demands of your classroom reading program as well as the other subjects you are required to teach. My own preference is to devote at least 20 to 30 minutes a day for three days a week to readers theatre. That suggestion is just that: a suggestion. You will need to decide how much time you can devote to this activity. It is important, however, that you use readers theatre as a regular and consistent teaching tool—not something dropped into the curriculum at odd times during the year or whenever you are searching for activities to fill time. The true value of readers theatre will come when students have regular, systematic opportunities to participate in and take advantage of all its components.

"Does readers theatre have any impact on students' comprehension development?"

As discussed throughout this book, there is a direct relationship between a regular program of readers theatre in the classroom and significant improvements in students' comprehension growth. Not only is there a wealth of research that supports this view, but observations of students and conversations with classroom teachers reveal that students often view readers theatre as "reading in action." Students become active participants who are engaged in meaningful activities that are both supportive and instructional. There is a significant difference between students circling the correct main idea on a photocopied page from the basal reader and students who present their own self-initiated version of "The Big Bad Wolf" to a receptive and enthusiastic audience. Comprehension is not just a by-product of readers theatre; it is one of its major goals and one of its major results.

"How can I make fluency a regular part of my reading program?"

Chapter 2 discussed several instructional methods that can be used to promote fluency development in your classroom. Most of these strategies can be easily and systematically incorporated into your regular language arts program or your overall reading curriculum. It is important for youngsters to understand that fluency is not just a simple skill that they must master for a standardized test, but rather a developmental process that all readers use and practice. By making fluency instruction a regular practice in your reading program you will be helping to underscore its value for all readers—irrespective of grade or ability.

"You seem to be pretty excited about readers theatre. Why?"

After nearly 40 years as an educator, I can't think of a more motivating strategy—for both students and teachers—than readers theatre. It promotes major elements of reading instruction (vocabulary, fluency, comprehension), it can be used in any subject area, it can be part of the language arts program of any grade, and it has significant application for readers at any level of reading proficiency. Most important, it puts reading in its proper context—an active engagement between reader and text!

"When will I begin seeing results (in fluency development) after I begin using readers theatre?"

It's important to remember that fluency doesn't just happen overnight. Like seeds in a garden, fluency needs time to germinate and grow. However, that said, my experience, and that of many teachers who have used readers theatre as a regular component of their classroom program, is that you will begin to see systematic improvements in approximately four to six weeks, subject to the varying ability levels in your classroom, the amount of time you devote to readers theatre on a daily or weekly basis, and the instructional goals of your classroom reading program.

"Won't students get tired of readers theatre if I use it all the time? How much is too much?"

Just like any classroom instructional activity you don't want to overuse readers theatre to the point that students grow tired of it. Consider using it systematically (but not exclusively) throughout the school year. If your reading series is divided into five units, for example, you may want to incorporate readers theatre into three of those five units. Perhaps you might incorporate readers theatre into your social studies program for the first and third marking periods of the year. Or you could consider readers theatre as the penultimate activity for any thematic unit you develop as part of your science program. In short, don't overuse it and don't abuse it. Listen carefully to your students. If they say, "Gee, that would be great story to turn into a readers theatre script," encourage them to pursue that. On the other hand, if you hear a chorus of groans when you announce readers theatre for the eleventh time in a week, you might consider some alternate plans.

"Won't parents think that readers theatre is more fun than instructional?"

For many parents, readers theatre may seem like a brand new instructional technique. They may not be familiar with the term and may not have participated in any readers theatre activities when they were students. Therefore, it is vital that you provide parents with lots of information about readers theatre throughout the school year. Letters, notes, classroom Web pages, e-mails, and other forms of communication are all important for informing parents and engaging them as supporters of readers theatre. Be sure to provide information (no "educationalese," please) on how readers theatre enhances fluency and comprehension. Let parents know how readers theatre enhances students' enthusiasm for and participation in a variety of subject areas. Sure, students will have lots of fun with readers theatre, but they will also demonstrate improved levels in all their language arts. Bottom line: Keep parents informed and you will always keep parents engaged.

"Will readers theatre help my ESL (English as a Second Language) students?"

As you may recall, readers theatre is an active form of repeated readings—the reading strategy in which students read a selection over and over again until they can do so with fluency and comprehension. For non-English-speaking students, readers theatre provides many opportunities to hear accomplished readers (their classmates) read a selection with proficiency. These proficient readers serve as positive models. In other words, more fluent students support less fluent classmates.

"What do I tell my principal?"

Try this: "Readers theatre has been demonstrated, through more than two decades of empirical research, to significantly improve students' vocabulary, fluency, and comprehension. This holds true for students at all levels of reading—irrespective of grade level. As an instructional activity, it supports almost all of the Reading/Language Arts Standards (11 of the 12) and is consistent with the overall goals of the school's reading program. It is motivational, energizing, and responsive to the individual needs of all students. Oh, it's also fun!"

Part III

Readers Theatre Scripts: Fables, Fantasies, and Fantastic Adventures

Fairy Tales

The Gingerbread Man

STAGING: The two narrators may stand at lecterns or podiums, one on either side of the staging area. The other characters may stand in a random pattern across the staging area. The Gingerbread Man may wish to move back and forth across the staging area each time he says, "Run, run, as fast as you can . . . ."

Cow	Horse	Thresher	Mower
X	X	X	X
Little Old Woman			Little Old Man
X			X
	Gingerbread Man		
	X	Fox	
		X	
Narrator 1			Narrator 2
X			X

NARRATOR 1: Once upon a time there was a Little Old Woman . . . .

LITTLE OLD WOMAN: That's me!

NARRATOR 2: . . . and a Little Old Man.

LITTLE OLD MAN: That's me!

NARRATOR 1: Well, they both lived alone in a little old house in the middle of the little old woods. They were very lonely, so one day the Little Old Woman decided to make a Gingerbread Boy.

NARRATOR 2: So she rolled out some gingerbread, sprinkled it with cinnamon, used some raisins for his eyes, and made his mouth out of rose-colored sugar. She put him on a pan and put him in the oven.

NARRATOR 1: After a time she opened the oven door and took out the pan.

LITTLE OLD WOMAN: That's what I did—I took out the pan!

LITTLE OLD MAN: Yes, she took out the pan.

NARRATOR 2: Just as she took out the pan, the little Gingerbread Boy jumped onto the floor and ran out the door.

NARRATOR 1: The Little Old Woman and the Little Old Man ran after the Gingerbread Boy. But the Gingerbread Boy was much too fast, and he ran down the road laughing and shouting.

GINGERBREAD BOY: Run, run, as fast as you can! You can't catch me, I'm the Gingerbread Man!

NARRATOR 2: And they couldn't catch him.

NARRATOR 1: The Gingerbread Boy ran down the road. Finally he came to a large field with a cow in it.

COW: Stop, little Gingerbread Boy. I want to eat you!

GINGERBREAD BOY: I have run away from a Little Old Man and a Little Old Woman, and I can run away from you, I can!

NARRATOR 2: The cow chased him down the road. But the Gingerbread Boy just looked over his shoulder and cried,

GINGERBREAD BOY: Run, run, as fast as you can! You can't catch me, I'm the Gingerbread Man!

NARRATOR 1: And the cow couldn't catch him.

NARRATOR 2: The little Gingerbread Boy ran on and on, until he came to a horse in a pasture.

HORSE: Please stop, Little Gingerbread Boy. You look good enough to eat.

GINGERBREAD BOY: Oh, no. I have run away from a Little Old Man and a Little Old Woman and a cow, and I can run away from you, I can!

NARRATOR 1: The horse chased him down the road. But the Gingerbread Boy just looked over his shoulder and cried,

GINGERBREAD BOY: Run, run, as fast as you can! You can't catch me, I'm the Gingerbread Man!

NARRATOR 2: And the horse couldn't catch him.

NARRATOR 1: By and by the little Gingerbread Boy came to a barn where a thresher was working.

THRESHER: Please stop, little Gingerbread Boy. You look good enough to eat.

GINGERBREAD BOY: Oh, no. I have run away from a Little Old Man and a Little Old Woman and a cow and a horse, and I can run away from you, I can!

NARRATOR 2: The thresher chased him down the road. But, the Gingerbread Boy just looked over his shoulder and cried,

GINGERBREAD BOY: Run, run, as fast as you can! You can't catch me, I'm the Gingerbread Man!

NARRATOR 1: And the thresher couldn't catch him.

NARRATOR 2: By and by the little Gingerbread Boy came to a field where a mower was working.

MOWER: Please stop, little Gingerbread Boy. You look good enough to eat.

GINGERBREAD BOY:	Oh, no. I have run away from a Little Old Man and a Little Old Woman and a cow and a horse and a thresher, and I can run away from you, I can!
NARRATOR 1:	The mower chased him down the road. But the Gingerbread Boy just looked over his shoulder and cried,
GINGERBREAD BOY:	Run, run, as fast as you can! You can't catch me, I'm the Gingerbread Man!
NARRATOR 2:	And the mower couldn't catch him.
NARRATOR 1:	By and by the little Gingerbread Boy came to a fox who was walking down the road.
GINGERBREAD BOY:	I have run away from a Little Old Man and a Little Old Woman and a cow and a horse and a thresher and a mower, and I can run away from you I can! Run, run, as fast as you can! You can't catch me, I'm the Gingerbread Man!
FOX:	Why, I am not interested in catching you. I would not think of such a thing!
NARRATOR 2:	Just then the little Gingerbread Boy came to a river. He could not swim across.
NARRATOR 1:	But he wanted to keep running away from all the animals and all the people who were chasing him.
FOX:	Hey, little Gingerbread Boy, why don't you jump on my tail and I will take you across the river?
NARRATOR 2:	So the little Gingerbread Boy jumped on the fox's tail, and the fox swam into the river. When he was a short distance from shore he turned his head and said,
FOX:	You are too heavy on my tail, little Gingerbread Boy. I'm afraid you will get wet. Why don't you jump on my back?
NARRATOR 1:	So the little Gingerbread Boy jumped on the fox's back.

NARRATOR 2: The fox swam a little farther out into the river and said to the little Gingerbread Boy,

FOX: I'm afraid the water will cover you there. Why don't you jump on my shoulder?

NARRATOR 1: So, the little Gingerbread Boy jumped on the fox's shoulder.

NARRATOR 2: In the middle of the river, the fox said to the little Gingerbread Boy,

FOX: Oh, no, my shoulder is sinking. Why don't you jump on my nose?

NARRATOR 1: So the little Gingerbread Boy jumped on the fox's . . .

NARRATOR 2: SNAP! SNAP! SNAP!

NARRATOR 1: And, just like that, the little Gingerbread Boy was gone!

NARRATOR 2: And he never ever said anything again.

FOX: Run, run, little Gingerbread Man.

I'm a hungry fox and I can eat you, I can!

Little Red Riding Hood

STAGING: The characters may stand at podiums or music stands. The Wolf and Red Riding Hood may wish to "walk" over to Granny and the Hunter for the later parts of the production. The narrator should be standing off to the side for the entire production.

	Little Red Riding Hood X	Wolf X		
Narrator X				
			Granny X	Hunter X

NARRATOR: We take you now to "Once Upon a Time" time. You know, the time that was a long, long time ago. It was a time before iPods and cell phones. It was a time before television and computers. It was a time when people used to walk through the woods to visit their grandmothers. And so, we introduce you to the person who is actually going to walk through the woods to

LITTLE RED RIDING HOOD: visit her grandmother . . . the hero of this story . . . Little Red Riding Hood.

LITTLE RED RIDING HOOD: That's right, I'm the hero, or more correctly, the heroine of this story. I'm not sure why the writer of this story gave me such a strange name, but maybe he just isn't as smart as some of us storybook characters. But anyway, enough about him. Let's get on with our story.

NARRATOR: So, one day Little Red Riding Hood decided that she wanted to go and visit her sweet grandmother. Now, you should know that Red's granny lived way on the other side of the forest . . . the deep dark forest . . . the very deep and the very dark forest. The very deep and very dark forest had all sorts of weird and strange creatures in it . . . like wolves and other critters who like nothing better than to scare little girls dressed up in red out for a little stroll in the forest.

WOLF: Hey, you know what? It always seems as though I'm the bad guy in all these stories. I don't understand why that is, but it just seems that I always have to growl or make a lot of noise or other such things so that you [points to audience] will think that I'm a mean and grouchy guy. I guess I'm just stuck with this part, so I guess I'll just do the best I can.

NARRATOR: So, let's get back to that day when Red Riding Hood decided to go and visit her poor old grandmother who lived on the other side of the deep and dark forest.

LITTLE RED RIDING HOOD: So, I went and packed a basket full of goodies—lots of potato salad, some fried chicken, cans of soda, a bag of cookies, and lots of napkins.

NARRATOR: She set out on the path that winds through the deep and dark forest. Now, as you might imagine, this was not going to be just a nice and easy trip through the forest. Noooooooooo. The writer person who made up this story thought that it should have a little action. And that's where our friend, the wolf, comes in.

WOLF: That's me!

NARRATOR: So Red Riding Hood was calmly walking through the forest. She stopped to tie her shoelaces. All of a sudden, from behind a tree, out steps the Big Bad Wolf.

LITTLE RED RIDING HOOD: Oh, you scared me.

WOLF: I'm sorry, I didn't mean to scare you. I guess this hairy face of mine isn't very pretty, but it's all I have.

LITTLE RED RIDING HOOD: That's okay, now that I can see you in the light, you're not that bad looking . . . I mean, for a wolf that is.

WOLF: Thanks. I guess a face like this would scare a lot of people, but you seem to be okay with it.

LITTLE RED RIDING HOOD: Yes, I am. So, what can I do for you, Mr. Big Bad Wolf?

WOLF: Well, according to the author of this story I'm supposed to scare you and run on ahead through the woods and meet you at your Granny's house.

LITTLE RED RIDING HOOD: That sounds like a good idea. Why don't you run on ahead, and I'll just skip along this path and pick flowers and sing a song, and then we can see what happens at the other end of the story?

WOLF:	Sounds great, Miss Hood. I'll see you later!
NARRATOR:	And so it was that the Big Bad Wolf ran on ahead to Granny's house. Little Red Riding Hood skipped on down the path, and in no time she was at her Granny's house, knocking on the door.
LITTLE RED RIDING HOOD:	Knock, knock, knock.
GRANNY:	Who's there?
LITTLE RED RIDING HOOD:	It's me, Granny. I have a basket filled with all kinds of goodies. I thought you might like to have a picnic.
GRANNY:	Well, why didn't you say so? Come right in.
NARRATOR:	Now, I guess I should tell you that Granny here [points to Granny] isn't the real Granny. This is actually a fake Granny. You see, the wolf in our story ran as fast as he could to Granny's house. When he got there he got to talking with Granny. You see, he and Granny are old friends. They used to go to high school together and hang out at the music store. Anyway, they decided to play a little joke on our friend Little Red Riding Hood. So the Big Bad Wolf climbed into some of Granny's clothes and pretended that he was Granny. Do you get it now? Okay, let's listen.
LITTLE RED RIDING HOOD:	My, Granny, what big ears you have.
GRANNY:	The better to listen to you, my dear.
LITTLE RED RIDING HOOD:	My, Granny, what big eyes you have.
GRANNY:	The better to see you, my dear.
LITTLE RED RIDING HOOD:	My, Granny, what big teeth you have.
GRANNY:	The better to eat you, my dear.

146

NARRATOR: With that, the wolf and the real Granny held on to Little Red Riding Hood and tickled her. Little Red Riding Hood laughed and laughed and laughed. They kept tickling her more and more. Her laughter rang through the woods and was heard by a hunter.

HUNTER: That's me!

NARRATOR: The hunter ran to Granny's house and burst in.

HUNTER: Hey, you two . . . stop tickling that little girl.

WOLF: Why should we listen to you?

HUNTER: Don't you know what time it is?

GRANNY: No, what time is it?

HUNTER: It's lunch time, and Little Red Riding Hood has this basket filled with all sorts of goodies. Why don't you just stop tickling her and we can have a great picnic together?

NARRATOR: And so Granny and the Wolf and Little Red Riding Hood and the Hunter all sat around Granny's living room and had a great picnic with lots of food, some good tunes, and lots of laughter (but no more tickling). And that's our story.

Legends and Folktales

The Leopard's Daughter

(Liberia)

STAGING: The two narrators may stand at lecterns or podiums, one on either side of the staging area. The other characters should be standing in a random pattern across the staging area. Selected characters (Elephant, Buffalo, Antelope) may wish to perform dancing motions ("Dance of War," "Dance of Peace") as necessary. Each should simulate a spear-throwing motion at the end of the dancing.

	Leopard	Elephant	Sir Buffalo	Dwarf Antelope	
	X	X	X	X	
Narrator 1					Narrator 2
X					X

NARRATOR 1: Long ago, in the country of Liberia there lived a leopard who was king of all the animals. He had many daughters, but there was one daughter who was the most beautiful of all.

NARRATOR 2: News of her beauty spread far and wide. All the other animals wanted to marry her because she was so beautiful. But the leopard did not like any of the suitors who came to court his daughter.

NARRATOR 1: Finally, he decided on a test to decide who would be the best husband for his daughter. So the next day the royal horns and the tribal drums called all the animals of the kingdom together into the middle of a great clearing. And the leopard spoke to them.

LEOPARD: Each of you has courted my daughter; each of you wants to be her husband. So I have created a test to see who will be the best husband for her. First each of you must do the Dance of War to show that you are strong and brave. Then you must do the Dance of Peace to show that there is kindness in your heart. Finally, you must take my royal spear and throw it into the air and count to 10 before it falls to the ground.

ELEPHANT: Is that it?

LEOPARD: Yes, that is what you must do.

SIR BUFFALO: That sounds like an easy test.

ELEPHANT: Then I will go first, because I am the biggest and strongest animal in the entire forest.

NARRATOR 1: And so the elephant danced the Dance of War to show that he was brave and strong.

[Elephant dances.]

Then he danced the Dance of Peace to show that there was kindness in his heart.

[Elephant dances.]

Finally, he took the Leopard's spear and threw it up into the air.

[Elephant makes throwing motion.]

But before he could get past the number six, the spear fell to the ground. The elephant failed the test.

SIR BUFFALO: Let me try. I am the next strongest animal in the forest.

NARRATOR 2: So it was that Sir Buffalo, the next strongest animal in the forest, tried the Leopard's test. He danced the Dance of War to show that he was brave.

[Sir Buffalo dances.]

Then he danced the Dance of Peace to show that there was kindness in his heart.

[Sir Buffalo dances.]

Then he took the Leopard's spear and threw it into the air.

[Sir Buffalo makes throwing motion.]

But before he could get past the number eight, the spear fell to the ground. Sir Buffalo had failed the test.

NARRATOR 1: Then all the other animals tried the test. But all the other animals failed. And they were all very angry as they began to walk away.

DWARF ANTELOPE: Please, let me try.

NARRATOR 2: It was then that everyone noticed the Dwarf Antelope—and they all began to laugh.

[Elephant and Sir Buffalo laugh.]

ELEPHANT: What makes you think you can pass the test?

SIR BUFFALO: You are the smallest animal.

DWARF ANTELOPE: I would like to try.

LEOPARD: We must be fair. We must give everyone a chance to do that test.

NARRATOR 1: And so the Dwarf Antelope stepped before all the other animals. He danced the Dance of War to show that he was strong and brave.

[Dwarf Antelope dances.]

He danced the Dance of Peace to show that there was kindness in his heart.

[Dwarf Antelope dances.]

Then he took the Leopard's spear in his mouth and threw it into the air.

[Dwarf Antelope makes throwing motion.]

DWARF ANTELOPE: Five plus five is ten!

NARRATOR 1: . . . and the spear clattered to the ground.

ELEPHANT: He cheated!

SIR BUFFALO: He did not play fair.

LEOPARD: No, my friends. All you were asked to do was to count to 10. I did not say HOW you were to make that count.

NARRATOR 2: And so it was that the Dwarf Antelope, the smallest animal in the entire forest, was able to marry the Leopard's daughter. And they both lived happily ever after.

NARRATOR 1: And the moral to this story is this: We should never judge an individual by how big or how strong he may be, but rather by how he uses his mind.

NARRATOR 2: And that is a folktale from the faraway country of Liberia, which is on the great continent of Africa.

Adapted from Anthony D. Fredericks, *African Legends, Myths, and Folktales for Readers Theatre* (Westport, CT: Teacher Ideas Press, 2008).

John Henry

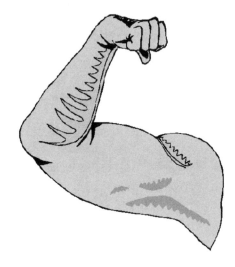

STAGING: The characters should all be at lecterns or podiums. John Henry should be placed in the center of the staging area. If possible, provide John Henry with a hammer to hold in one hand throughout the presentation. The chorus should be placed to the rear of the staging area.

```
                        Chorus
                      X   X   X
             Polly Ann              Captain Tommy
                 X                        X
      Man                John Henry
       X                     X
Narrator 1                                   Narrator 2
   X                                             X
```

CHORUS: Oh, my hammer,
Hammer ring,
While I sing, Lawd,
Hear me sing!

NARRATOR 1: There's this story—a true story I hear tell—been around the hills of West Virginia for many years. It's the story of John Henry—John Henry, the best steel driving man in the whole country.

NARRATOR 2: Yup, that steel drivin' man was the best there ever was. He could hammer for hours without missing a beat. He could hammer better and faster than any four men put together. His hammer was so fast he had to cool it down with a bucket of water every 15 minutes just so a fire wouldn't start.

NARRATOR 1: All the railroad bosses wanted John Henry to work for them 'cause he was the best there ever was. Yes, he was the best there ever was.

CHORUS: Ain't no hammer.
Rings like mine,
Rings like gold, Lawd,
Ain't it fine?

Rings like silver,
Peal on peal,
Into the rock, Lawd,
Drive the steel.

If'n I dies, Lawd,
I command,
Bury the hammer
In my hand.

NARRATOR 2: Well, one day the old Chesapeake and Ohio Railroad started making a tunnel in the Allegheny Mountains. The boss man—Captain Tommy—wanted the best there was. He wanted John Henry to work for him.

CAPTAIN TOMMY: John Henry, I hear that you're the best steel drivin' man there is.

JOHN HENRY: You heard right. I'm the biggest, the strongest, and the best steel drivin' man there ever was. What you heard is true.

CAPTAIN TOMMY: Then I want you to work for me. I want you to lead the men through the mountain. I want you to build me a tunnel through this mountain so that the train can come through here on its way to the great wild west. John Henry, I want you to build me a tunnel.

JOHN HENRY: That I will, boss, that I will.

NARRATOR 1: So John Henry picked up, not one, but two steel hammers—one in each hand—and he commenced to swinging. He commenced to swinging so hard and so fast that the tunnel was five feet into the mountain before the lunch bell rang. But John Henry didn't stop for lunch. No, he continued to work. He continued to swing those hammers. He continued to build that tunnel. Yep, he was the best steel driving man there ever was.

CHORUS: Oh, my hammer,
Hammer ring,
While I sing, Lawd,
Hear me sing!

NARRATOR 2: Now, that was a hot summer. It was a hot summer in West Virginia that year. Men dropped like flies in the summer heat. But not John Henry. John Henry jus' kept swinging those hammers through the heat of the day. While other men took a break, John Henry—his muscles rippling all across his body—jus' kept swinging those hammers. Yup, John Henry was a steel drivin' man.

NARRATOR 1: Well, one day in the heat of the August sun a man appeared at the entrance to the tunnel. He had a machine with him, a special machine.

MAN: Hey, come on, everybody I got me a special machine. This here's a steam drill. It can drill holes faster than a dozen men working together. Yes sir, this here's the best thing that's ever happened in these here parts.

CAPTAIN TOMMY: I jus' don't know 'bout that. I got me the best steel drivin' man in seven counties workin' right here. I got me John Henry working on this tunnel. Yup, John Henry, why he could beat a dozen men workin' together. He's the best there ever was.

MAN: That sounds impossible. Nobody's that good! But I'll tell you what, if Mr. John Henry is faster than my steam driller, I'll give you this here machine for free.

CAPTAIN TOMMY: Hey, John Henry, this man says that his machine is better than you. He says his machine can work faster than you. He thinks his machine is better than you. What do you say to a contest?

NARRATOR 2: Now John Henry wasn't just the strongest man in seven counties, he was a pretty smart man, too. As he looked at that steam machine he saw the future. He saw a whole lot of steam machines drillin' tunnels all across the U.S. of A. He saw a whole bunch of steam machines puttin' he and his friends out of work. He saw men out of jobs, out of work, and out of luck. He knew he had to do something to save his friends and their jobs.

JOHN HENRY: I'll take that challenge. I'd rather die with a hammer in my hand than let some steam drillin' machine beat me down.

CHORUS: Ain't no hammer.
Rings like mine,
Rings like gold, Lawd,
Ain't it fine?

Rings like silver,
Peal on peal,
Into the rock, Lawd,
Drive the steel.

If'n I dies, Lawd,
I command,
Bury the hammer
In my hand.

NARRATOR 1: Soon as word got out 'bout the contest 'tween John Henry and the steam machine, people came from miles around to see it with their own eyes. Yup, it was another hot day in the West Virginia hills as John Henry and the steam machine stood side by side waitin' for the big race to start.

NARRATOR 2: Then "BANG," the race was on! At first the steam drill drove the steel twice as fast as John Henry. But John Henry picked up another hammer in his hand and commenced to working with two hammers. Blow after blow he struck away at the side of the mountain. Blow after blow he cut into the side of the mountain.

NARRATOR 1: Faster and faster John Henry drilled into the side of the mountain. Faster and faster John Henry moved in front of the steam drill. John Henry's hammer sounded like ten thousand hammers echoing throughout the tunnel. For six hours . . . seven hours . . . eight hours he hammered his way into the mountain . . . he hammered his way in front of the steam drill.

NARRATOR 2: The crowd cheered. The crowd screamed. John Henry could not be stopped. Each of his hammers glowed white-hot as he tunneled deeper and deeper into the mountain. He was drivin' that steel faster and better than any machine.

CHORUS: Oh, my hammer,
Hammer ring,
While I sing, Lawd,
Hear me sing!

NARRATOR 1: Finally, at the ninth hour of the contest the steam drill jus' up and broke down. It was all over. The contest was over.

CAPTAIN TOMMY: I proclaim John Henry the winner of the contest. Ol' John Henry beat that steam machine. He beat that steam drill fair and square. He went farther into the mountain than the steam drill. He is the best! He is the best there ever was!

NARRATOR 2: The crowd cheered! The crowd yelled! But when they quieted down, they heard another sound. They heard a scream. It was the scream of Polly Ann—John Henry's wife.

POLLY ANN: John Henry, John Henry. John Henry, don't go!

NARRATOR 1: John Henry lay on the ground. His heart had burst. His blood ran red over the dirt.

POLLY ANN: John Henry, John Henry. John Henry, don't go!

JOHN HENRY: A man ain't nothin' but a man. Fore I let that steam drill beat me, I'll die with a hammer in my hand. Yes, I will. I'll die with a hammer in my hand.

NARRATOR 2: That day, they carried John Henry down from the mountain. They carried him to the river and buried him with a hammer in each hand and a rod of steel across his chest. They put a pick and shovel at his head and they put a pick and shovel at his feet. That day, they buried the best steel drivin' man there ever was. Yup, they buried the best steel drivin' man there ever was!

CHORUS: Ain't no hammer.
Rings like mine,
Rings like gold, Lawd,
Ain't it fine?

Rings like silver,
Peal on peal,
Into the rock, Lawd,
Drive the steel.

If'n I dies, Lawd,
I command,
Bury the hammer
In my hand . . .
Yes, bury the hammer
In my hand.

Adapted from Anthony D. Fredericks, *American Folklore, Legends, and Tall Tales for Readers Theatre* (Westport, CT: Teacher Ideas Press, 2008).

Monkey and Crocodiles

(Cameroon)

STAGING: The narrator may stand at a podium or lectern. The three crocodiles should stand in a straight line (each at a music stand or small table). The monkey may walk around between the other characters. You may wish to lay some blue ribbons on the floor to simulate a river.

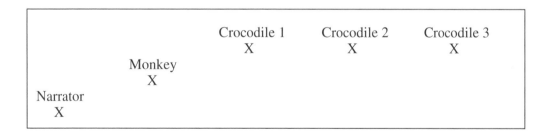

		Crocodile 1 X	Crocodile 2 X	Crocodile 3 X
	Monkey X			
Narrator X				

NARRATOR: Once upon a time, there was a small village. Near the village was a very wide river. The water in the river flowed swiftly. But on the other side of the river there was a banana plantation rich with many bananas. It was said that the bananas were the best in all the land and were much prized. People from all over loved those bananas and would talk about them with much affection.

MONKEY: I, too, like those bananas. I would like to have some bananas to eat. They are very good, and I should like to have some for myself. I think I will go and get myself some excellent bananas.

NARRATOR: And so the monkey packed his bag and set out for the banana plantation. But first he came to the very wide river. He had to get across the river in order to get to the bananas he prized so much. The river was very wide and very swift. And the monkey could not swim.

MONKEY: I do not know how to swim. How will I get across?

NARRATOR: The monkey sat down on the side of the river and thought and thought and thought. After a long time thinking he came up with a plan . . . a very brilliant plan. He looked across the river and soon spied a crocodile swimming in the river.

MONKEY: Oh, my brother crocodile. You look very happy swimming in the river. I hope everything is good for you.

CROCODILE 1: Oh, yes it is. It is a very fine day, and I am a very happy crocodile.

MONKEY: I am so pleased to hear that my brother is happy today.

CROCODILE 1: Yes, I am. Perhaps you would like to join me. Perhaps you would like to swim with me, and we can enjoy this fine day together.

NARRATOR: But the monkey was a very wise monkey. He knew that if he even put his foot in the river the crocodile would immediately eat him up.

MONKEY: I would love to swim with you, my brother. But why should we have all the fun? Why don't we invite all your family?

CROCODILE 1: That is a very good idea indeed.

CROCODILE 2: Yes, that is a very good idea. We should all swim together and enjoy this very fine day!

CROCODILE 3:	Yes, I agree. It will be a great day all around.
MONKEY:	That is so true, my brothers. But I am wondering how many there are of you. How many of your family are in this river? How many would I be swimming with?
CROCODILE 2:	There are many of us.
CROCODILE 3:	We are a very big family. A very big family indeed!
CROCODILE 1:	We are such a large family that nobody can count all of us.
MONKEY:	You may not believe me, but I can count. I can count very well. I will count all of you, and then we will know how many of you there are.
CROCODILE 2:	Can you believe that? A monkey who can count!
CROCODILE 3:	I don't believe it! I don't think a monkey can count.
MONKEY:	It is true. I can count very well. Very well indeed!
CROCODILE 1:	Well, then let us see for ourselves.
ALL CROCODILES:	Brothers! Sisters! Come out! Come out!
NARRATOR:	All the crocodiles poked their heads out of the water. They all looked at the monkey.
MONKEY:	So that I may count all of you, you must line up from one bank of the river to the other. You must all be together from one side of the river to the other side. That is the only way I can count you. That is the only way to know how many of you there are.
NARRATOR:	So all the crocodiles lined up. They lined up from one bank of the river to the other bank. Then the monkey started walking on the crocodiles' backs. As he walked, he started counting them.
MONKEY:	[slowly moving in front of the crocodiles] 1, 2, 3, 4, 5 . . . .
NARRATOR:	When he was about halfway across the backs of the crocodiles, he nearly fell into the water.

163

MONKEY: Be still, my friends. I want to be sure to count each one of you.

CROCODILE 1: We will be still.

CROCODILE 2: Yes, we will not move.

CROCODILE 3: We want you to count each one of us.

NARRATOR: And so the monkey continued his count as he made his way across the backs of all the crocodiles.

MONKEY: 57, 58, 59, 60 . . . .

NARRATOR: Finally the monkey reached the last crocodile and was about to leap onto the other bank of the river.

CROCODILE 1: Wait! Get hold of the monkey.

CROCODILE 2: He is going to jump away.

CROCODILE 3: He is going to get across the river.

NARRATOR: But it was already too late. The monkey jumped from the back of the last crocodile onto the other river bank. He had succeeded in getting across the river.

MONKEY: Ha, ha, ha. My little plan worked. Good-bye, my brothers. Thank you for giving me a bridge across the wide river. Perhaps I shall see you again on another journey.

ALL CROCODILES: We've been tricked!

NARRATOR: And the monkey traveled to the banana plantation and had himself a great feast of delicious bananas.

ALL CROCODILES: We've been tricked!

NARRATOR: This story reminds us that you don't have to be big and strong to succeed in life. You just have to be a little bit smarter than others who would do you in.

Adapted from Anthony D. Fredericks, *African Legends, Myths, and Folktales for Readers Theatre* (Westport, CT: Teacher Ideas Press, 2008).

Nonfiction and Informal

It's Alive

(Living and Nonliving Things)

STAGING: The narrator stands in the front and to the side of the staging area. The other characters are seated around a table on which several items have been placed. As each character speaks, she or he will pick up a designated object and hold it so that the audience can clearly see it.

	Bob X		Sarah X
		(table)	
	Clifton X		Kasha X
Narrator X			

NARRATOR: Good morning. Welcome to our science class. We have a puzzle. Let's see if it can be solved.

BOB: [holds rock] What is this thing?

CLIFTON: It's a rock.

BOB: How do you know?

CLIFTON: Because it's not alive.

BOB: Not alive. What do you mean?

KASHA: I know. It's not alive because it can't grow.

SARAH: That's right. All living things grow.

BOB: Are trees living things?

CLIFTON: Yes. Trees are living because they grow.

BOB: What else?

KASHA: [holds a plant] This plant is a living thing.

BOB: Why?

SARAH: It's a living thing because it grows. It's also a living thing because it needs water and air to grow.

BOB: So, if something needs water to grow, then it must be a living thing.

KASHA: That's right, Bob.

BOB: [holds photo of elephant] Let's see. This elephant can grow.

CLIFTON: That's right.

BOB: And this elephant needs water.

SARAH: That's right.

BOB: So that means that this elephant is a living thing.

ALL: THAT'S RIGHT!

BOB: What else do I need to know?

KASHA: Well, living things have parents.

BOB: Do all living things have parents?

CLIFTON: Yes, they do. Elephant babies have parents. Plants make seeds. The seeds grow into new plants. And children have parents.

BOB: So that means that all of us [points] are living things?

ALL: THAT'S RIGHT!

BOB: Okay, let's see what how this works. [holds up toy car] This is not a living thing because it doesn't grow.

SARAH: And it doesn't need water.

KASHA: And it doesn't have parents.

BOB: THAT'S RIGHT!

CLIFTON: Hey Bob. What about you?

BOB: Am I a living thing? Let's see. I need water. I grow. And, I have parents. That means I'm a living thing.

ALL: THAT'S RIGHT!

Adapted from Anthony D. Fredericks, *Nonfiction Readers Theatre for Beginning Readers* (Westport, CT: Teacher Ideas Press, 2007).

Water, Water Everywhere

(Water)

STAGING: There is no narrator for this script. The four characters may be seated on stools or on chairs.

	Vicky X		Julie X	
Mark X				Mike X

MARK: You know, I was reading about water in a library book.

VICKY: Okay, what did you learn?

MARK: I learned that most of the earth is covered by water.

JULIE: Wow, that's cool. That must be a lot of water.

MIKE: Yes, it is. I heard that more than three-quarters of the earth has water on it.

VICKY: That doesn't leave a lot of room for the land.

MIKE: No, it doesn't.

MARK: But did you know that there are two kinds of water?

JULIE: Two kinds! Let's see. Isn't one kind of water called fresh water?

MIKE: That's right. Fresh water is the water in rivers and streams.

VICKY: Yes, and fresh water is the water in rain and snow.

JULIE: Lakes also have fresh water.

MARK: Here's something amazing. Most fresh water is locked up.

JULIE: What do you mean "locked up?"

MARK: Well, most fresh water is locked up in icebergs.

MIKE: You mean those big giant things at the South Pole?

MARK: Right!

VICKY: And there are icebergs at the North Pole, too.

MIKE: But there is also lots of fresh water in the ground, too.

VICKY: Right. Most of the water in the ground comes from rain and snow.

MARK: When water is in the ground, it's called "groundwater."

VICKY: Well, duh!

MARK: Hey, smarty pants, do you know why groundwater is important?

JULIE: Hey, yourself. I know why it's important. Lots of people get their drinking water from the ground.

MIKE: That's right. They dig wells and pump the water up.

VICKY: But there's something else that's amazing about water.

MARK: What's that?

VICKY: Most of the water in the world is salt water. It's called salt water because it has lots of salt in it.

JULIE: That means that fresh water doesn't have salt.

MIKE: Right!

VICKY: Wait! I know. Most of the salt water in the world is in oceans.

MIKE: Right again!

VICKY: It's the oceans that cover three-quarters of the earth.

MIKE: Right! Right! Right!

JULIE: So we know that there is lots of fresh water.

MIKE: And we know there is lots of salt water.

MARK: Yes, there's water, water everywhere.

VICKY: Water in the lakes,
Water in the sea.
Some is for the little fish,
And some is for me!

Adapted from Anthony D. Fredericks, *Nonfiction Readers Theatre for Beginning Readers* (Westport, CT: Teacher Ideas Press, 2007).

Under One Rock

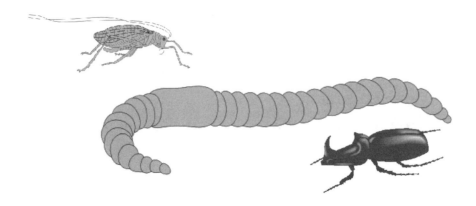

NOTE: The following script is based on the children's book *Under One Rock: Bugs, Slugs and Other Ughs* by Anthony D. Fredericks (Nevada City, CA: Dawn Publications, 2001). It serves as an example of how a piece of children's literature (in this case, nonfiction literature) can be developed into a readers theatre script (see chapter 7) for classroom production.

STAGING: The narrators sit on stools behind the characters. The characters may sit in chairs or stand. Place a rock of considerable size in the middle of the staging area.

Narrator 1						Narrator 2
X						X
Earthworm	Ant	Spider	Beetle	Cricket	Millipede	Slug
X	X	X	X	X	X	X
			(rock)			

NARRATOR 1: Here is a field for insects to play in,
And acres of shade for turtles to lay in;

NARRATOR 2: With wind-brushed trees for birds to nest in,
And sun-splashed spaces for lizards to rest in.

NARRATOR 1: This is where, on this summer day,
There lay a rock, all rough and gray.

NARRATOR 2: This is the rock [points].

NARRATOR 1: The rough-gray rock was discovered by chance,
By a brown-skinned boy in ragged pants,

NARRATOR 2: A curious lad who wondered aloud,
"What could be hiding in the red rich ground?"

NARRATOR 1: He lifted the rock, all rough and gray,
That he saw in the field on that summer's day.

NARRATOR 2: And there he found some varied creatures,
A village of animals with special features.

EARTHWORM: I am an earthworm all squiggly and round.
I aerate the soil in the red rich ground.

NARRATOR 1: Below the big rock, all rough and gray,

NARRATOR 2: That hides a whole crowd on a summer's day.

ANT: This is my family of hundreds of ants.
We dig twisting tunnels and farm tiny plants.

NARRATOR 1: Below the big rock, all rough and gray,

NARRATOR 2: That hides a whole crowd on a summer's day.

SPIDER: I am the spider with my eight-eyed face.
I build a sweet home in this cool dark place.

NARRATOR 1: Below the big rock, all rough and gray,

NARRATOR 2: That hides a whole crowd on a summer's day.

BEETLE: I am a beetle all shiny and black,
With grooves running down both sides of my back.

NARRATOR 1: Below the big rock, all rough and gray,

NARRATOR 2: That hides a whole crowd on a summer's day.

CRICKET: I'm a tiny field cricket who sings with my feet.
I search near the rock for some seeds I can eat.

NARRATOR 1: Below the big rock, all rough and gray,

NARRATOR 2: That hides a whole crowd on a summer's day.

MILLIPEDE: I'm a sole millipede with a sensitive feel.
I slip through the dirt in search of a meal.

NARRATOR 1: Below the big rock, all rough and gray,

NARRATOR 2: That hides a whole crowd on a summer's day.

SLUG: I'm a tiny slug all covered with slime.
I creep over soil, eating most of the time.

NARRATOR 1: Below the big rock, all rough and gray,

NARRATOR 2: That hides a whole crowd on a summer's day.

EARTHWORM: The creatures and critters

ANT: Live together as one,

SPIDER: Beneath the gray rock,

BEETLE: Away from the sun.

CRICKET: A collection of neighbors,

MILLIPEDE: The large and the small;

SLUG: And the place where they live,

ALL: Is home to them all.

Songs and Rhymes

If You're Happy and You Know It

STAGING: The characters should all be standing. They should be encouraged to interact with the audience as much as possible (pointing, walking toward the audience, etc.). The narrator may also be standing or placed at a lectern or music stand.

```
                                                              Narrator
                                                                 X
                Cassie              Lamanda
                  X                    X
    Jerrill                                       Juan
       X                                            X
```

NARRATOR: Is everybody happy?

JERRILL: I'm happy!

CASSIE: I'm happy, too.

LAMANDA: I'm very, very happy.

JUAN: It looks like everybody here is happy. What about them? [points to audience]

NARRATOR: Well, folks, are you all happy?

AUDIENCE: YES!

NARRATOR: Well, it looks like everybody here is happy.

JERRILL: Hey, I have a question. How do we know when someone is happy?

LAMANDA: Well, if she is smiling, then she must be happy.

CASSIE: Yeah, that's right—when people smile, then they are happy.

JERRILL: Can someone be happy and not smile?

JUAN: I guess so.

LAMANDA: How would he show it?

JERRILL: What do you mean?

LAMANDA: Can someone be happy and not be smiling?

CASSIE: I guess he could. But how would you know?

JUAN: I guess if he was singing, then he would be happy.

LAMANDA: That sounds right. If he was dancing, then he would be happy.

JERRILL: That sounds right. How else could someone be happy?

CASSIE: Maybe if she was cheering or shouting, then she would be happy.

JUAN: That sounds right.

LAMANDA: Well, maybe we should ask the audience. [points to audience]

NARRATOR: Okay, audience, are you ready to show us how you are happy?

AUDIENCE: YES! YES! YES!

NARRATOR: Okay, let's go!

[Consider playing the music for the remainder of this script.]

CASSIE: If you're happy and you know it, clap your hands.

AUDIENCE: [clap clap]

LAMANDA: If you're happy and you know it, clap your hands.

AUDIENCE: [clap clap]

JERRILL: If you're happy and you know it, then your face will surely show it.

JUAN: If you're happy and you know it, clap your hands.

AUDIENCE: [clap clap]

CASSIE: If you're happy and you know it, stomp your feet.

AUDIENCE: [stomp stomp]

LAMANDA: If you're happy and you know it, stomp your feet.

AUDIENCE: [stomp stomp]

JERRILL: If you're happy and you know it, then your face will surely show it.

JUAN: If you're happy and you know it, stomp your feet.

AUDIENCE: [stomp stomp]

CASSIE: If you're happy and you know it, shout "Hurray!"

AUDIENCE: HOO-RAY!

LAMANDA: If you're happy and you know it, shout "Hurray!"

AUDIENCE: HOO-RAY!

JERRILL: If you're happy and you know it, then your face will surely show it.

JUAN: If you're happy and you know it, shout "Hurray!"

AUDIENCE: HOO-RAY!

CASSIE: If you're happy and you know it, do all three.

AUDIENCE: [clap clap, stomp stomp] HOO-RAY!

LAMANDA: If you're happy and you know it, do all three.

AUDIENCE: [clap clap, stomp stomp] HOO-RAY!

JERRILL: If you're happy and you know it, then your face will surely show it.

JUAN: If you're happy and you know it, do all three.

AUDIENCE: [clap clap, stomp stomp] HOO-RAY!

Adapted from Anthony D. Fredericks, *Songs and Rhymes Readers Theatre for Beginning Readers* (Westport, CT: Teacher Ideas Press, 2007).

Humpty Dumpty

STAGING: The characters may be seated on stools or chairs. They may also be standing or placed at individual lecterns.

Girl 1	Girl 2	Boy 1	Boy 2	Big Bad Wolf
X	X	X	X	X

GIRL 1: Hello, Audience. [waves to the audience]

GIRL 2: Yes, hello Audience. [waves to audience]

BOY 1: We are happy to be here!

BOY 2: Yes, we have a funny story to share.

BIG BAD WOLF: Grumble, grumble, grumble.

GIRL 1: Hey, why is the Big Bad Wolf in this story?

GIRL 2: I don't know. Do you know? [points to Boy 1]

BOY 1: I don't know. Do you know? [points to Boy 2]

BOY 2: I don't know why he is here. He sure looks strange.

BIG BAD WOLF:	Yeah, why am I here? I think the author made a big mistake.
GIRL 1:	What do you mean?
BIG BAD WOLF:	I don't think the writer of this story is very smart.
GIRL 2:	Yeah, you're right. Isn't this a story about a big egg?
BOY 1:	Yes, it is. It's a story about a big egg, not a big bad wolf.
BIG BAD WOLF:	Yeah, I don't get it. Maybe the author went to sleep when he was writing this story.
BOY 2:	Yeah, I don't think the writer was paying attention.
BIG BAD WOLF:	So, is it okay if I leave?
GIRL 1:	I guess so.
GIRL 2:	I think it's okay.
BOY 1:	What about the writer?
BIG BAD WOLF:	I wouldn't listen to him any more. He doesn't know what he is doing.
BOY 2:	I think you're right.
GIRL 1:	So, I guess you can leave.
BIG BAD WOLF:	I think I'll go over to another story.
GIRL 2:	Which one?
BIG BAD WOLF:	I think there's a story about some pigs. I think they try to build houses. One of the pigs isn't very smart.
BOY 1:	Oh, you mean like the writer of this story.
BIG BAD WOLF:	Yeah, just like the writer.
BOY 2:	Okay, we'll see you later.
BIG BAD WOLF:	Yeah. See you later. [The "Wolf" exits offstage.]
GIRL 1:	Now we can do our story. Is everybody ready?
ALL:	Yes.

GIRL 1: Then, let's go. Humpty Dumpty . . .

GIRL 2: . . . sat on a wall.

BOY 1: Humpty Dumpty . . .

BOY 2: . . . had a great fall

GIRL 1: All the . . .

GIRL 2: . . . king's horses

BOY 1: And all . . .

BOY 2: . . . the king's men

GIRL 1: Couldn't . . .

GIRL 2: . . . put Humpty . . .

BOY 1: . . . together . . .

BOY 2: . . . again.

GIRL 1: Hey, that was very good.

GIRL 2: Yes, you're right.

BOY 1: And, you know what?

BOY 2: What?

BOY 1: We didn't need that old Big Bad Wolf.

GIRL 1: Yeah, we didn't need the wolf at all.

GIRL 2: I hope he found another story.

BOY 1: I hope he did, too.

BOY 2: I think he did. But I'm a little worried about those pigs.

Adapted from Anthony D. Fredericks, *Mother Goose Readers Theatre for Beginning Readers* (Westport, CT: Teacher Ideas Press, 2007).

The Ants Go Marching

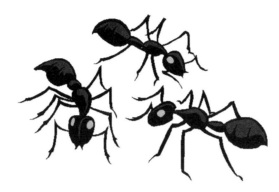

STAGING: This script is designed to allow for maximum participation by all members of the class. All students should be standing. As each part comes up, the designated number of students come to the front of the room, turn around to face the rest of the class, say their lines, and perform their parts For example, for "The ants go marching one by one," one student stands in front of the others and says her or his lines while marching in place during the singing of that verse. For "The ants go marching two by two," two students get up, speak, and "march" in front of the class as that verse is being sung. This continues throughout the song until the very end, when all the students in the class jump up and shout, "THE END."

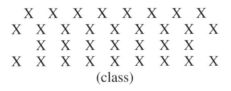

ONE STUDENT: The ants go marching one by one, [in front of class]

CLASS: Hurrah, hurrah!

ONE STUDENT: The ants go marching one by one,

CLASS: Hurrah, hurrah!

ONE STUDENT: The ants go marching one by one,
The little one stops to suck his thumb.
And they all go marching

CLASS: Down to the ground,
To get out of the rain,
BOOM! BOOM! BOOM!

TWO STUDENTS: The ants go marching two by two, [in front of class]

CLASS: Hurrah, hurrah!

TWO STUDENTS: The ants go marching two by two,

CLASS: Hurrah, hurrah!

TWO STUDENTS: The ants go marching two by two,
The little one stops to tie his shoe.
And they all go marching

CLASS: Down to the ground,
To get out of the rain,
BOOM! BOOM! BOOM!

THREE STUDENTS: The ants go marching three by three, [in front of class]

CLASS: Hurrah, hurrah!

THREE STUDENTS: The ants go marching three by three,

CLASS: Hurrah, hurrah!

THREE STUDENTS: The ants go marching three by three,
The little one stops to climb a tree
And they all go marching

CLASS: Down to the ground
To get out of the rain,
BOOM! BOOM! BOOM!

FOUR STUDENTS: The ants go marching four by four, [in front of class]

CLASS: Hurrah, hurrah!

FOUR STUDENTS: The ants go marching four by four,

CLASS: Hurrah, hurrah!

FOUR STUDENTS: The ants go marching four by four,
The little one stops to shut the door.
And they all go marching

184

CLASS:	Down to the ground, To get out of the rain, BOOM! BOOM! BOOM!
FIVE STUDENTS:	The ants go marching five by five, [in front of class]
CLASS:	Hurrah, hurrah!
FIVE STUDENTS:	The ants go marching five by five,
CLASS:	Hurrah, hurrah!
FIVE STUDENTS:	The ants go marching five by five, The little one stops to take a dive. And they all go marching
CLASS:	Down to the ground, To get out of the rain, BOOM! BOOM! BOOM!
SIX STUDENTS:	The ants go marching six by six, [in front of class]
CLASS:	Hurrah, hurrah!
SIX STUDENTS:	The ants go marching six by six,
CLASS:	Hurrah, hurrah!
SIX STUDENTS:	The ants go marching six by six, The little one stops to pick up sticks. And they all go marching
CLASS:	Down to the ground, To get out of the rain, BOOM! BOOM! BOOM!
SEVEN STUDENTS:	The ants go marching seven by seven, [in front of class]
CLASS:	Hurrah, hurrah!
SEVEN STUDENTS:	The ants go marching seven by seven,
CLASS:	Hurrah, hurrah!
SEVEN STUDENTS:	The ants go marching seven by seven, The little one stops to pray to heaven. And they all go marching
CLASS:	Down to the ground, To get out of the rain, BOOM! BOOM! BOOM!

EIGHT STUDENTS: The ants go marching eight by eight, [in front of class]

CLASS: Hurrah, hurrah!

EIGHT STUDENTS: The ants go marching eight by eight,

CLASS: Hurrah, hurrah!

EIGHT STUDENTS: The ants go marching eight by eight,
The little one stops to shut the gate.
And they all go marching

CLASS: Down to the ground,
To get out of the rain,
BOOM! BOOM! BOOM!

NINE STUDENTS: The ants go marching nine by nine, [in front of class]

CLASS: Hurrah, hurrah!

NINE STUDENTS: The ants go marching nine by nine,

CLASS: Hurrah, hurrah!

NINE STUDENTS: The ants go marching nine by nine,
The little one stops to check the time.
And they all go marching

CLASS: Down to the ground,
To get out of the rain,
BOOM! BOOM! BOOM!

TEN STUDENTS: The ants go marching ten by ten, [in front of class]

CLASS: Hurrah, hurrah!

TEN STUDENTS: The ants go marching ten by ten,

CLASS: Hurrah, hurrah!

TEN STUDENTS: The ants go marching ten by ten,
The little one stops to say,

CLASS: "THE END"

Adapted from Anthony D. Fredericks, *Songs and Rhymes Readers Theatre for Beginning Readers* (Westport, CT: Teacher Ideas Press, 2007).

Historical and Realistic Fiction

Long Hours, Long Days

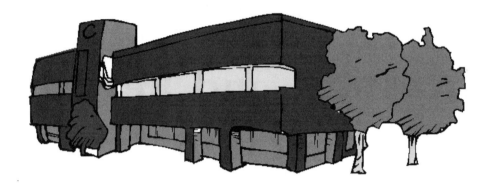

STAGING: The characters may all be seated on stools or chairs in the center of the staging area. Each worker can be simulating the movement of her or his work (for example, the man may be moving sheets of paper representing leather strips from one pile to another; the woman may pretend to be working a sewing machine, etc.). The narrator/interviewer is at a lectern or podium at the side of the staging area.

	Man	Woman	Child 1	Child 2
	X	X	X	X
Narrator/Interviewer				
X				

NARRATOR: During the late 1800s many new machines were invented. These machines helped change the face of American industry. Machines such as the typewriter, the telephone, the electric light bulb, the cash register, the fountain pen, the adding machine, and the vacuum cleaner made life easier and production more efficient. Other machines helped people do their jobs faster. More goods could be produced in less time.

These new inventions helped businesses grow and stimulated the growth of brand new industries. More factories were built, and more people were needed to operate the machines in those factories. There seemed to be plenty of work for everyone. But all was not as rosy as it seemed. Let's ask our workers here some questions.

INTERVIEWER: Tell us, sir, where do you work?

MAN: [slowly and sadly] I work in a shoe factory, a very large shoe factory. I work along with 2,000 other people in a very large and very dark factory. I work for 15 hours a day at a machine that sews the upper part of a shoe to the sole of the shoe. The machine can do this work very quickly. All I do is put the leather into the machine, and the machine sews the parts together. Then I take that part of the shoe out of the machine, put it in a box, and put another piece of leather into the machine.

INTERVIEWER: How long do you work each day?

MAN: I do my work over and over and over again. Just put a piece of leather in the machine and take a sewn piece of leather out of the machine. One piece of leather every 90 seconds. One piece goes in and one piece comes out, every 90 seconds. That's 40 times every hour. Every hour I put in 40 pieces of leather. Every hour I take out 40 pieces of leather. I do that every day for 15 hours every day. That's 600 pieces of leather to put into the machine every day. That's 600 pieces of leather to take out of the machine every day. Every day, 600 pieces of leather for 600 shoes. 600 shoe parts every day.

INTERVIEWER: How many days a week do you work?

MAN: I work for six days every week. Every week I work from Monday through Saturday. Six days a week, 15 hours every day. That's 90 hours every week. Ninety hours a week putting pieces of leather into a machine and taking pieces of leather out of a machine. Hour after hour, day after day, week after week. Always doing the same thing. Always standing in the same place. Always doing the same thing. Time after time, day after day, week after week. That's all I do. That's my job. My job is feeding a machine pieces of leather. All the time feeding a machine pieces of leather. Over and over and over and over. That's my job.

NARRATOR: The "sameness" of factory work was everywhere. Both men and women worked in factories, often doing repetitive jobs for very low wages. But in many cities, factory jobs were the only jobs available, particularly for unskilled workers.

INTERVIEWER: Excuse me, ma'am. Could you please tell us about your work?

WOMAN: [dejectedly] I work in a shirt factory with many other people. There are many of us in that factory, many of us working together sewing shirts. We sew shirts together. We get pieces of cloth. We put pieces of cloth into sewing machines. We sew. We sew the pieces of cloth together for part of a shirt. All day long we sew shirts. We do nothing else but sew shirts. That's what I do. I sew shirts. I sew shirts and so do the other 450 people in this factory. I sew collars on shirts. Every day I come to work I know what my job is going to be. I know I will sew collars on shirts. Every day I sew collars. It takes me two minutes to sew a collar on a shirt. I can sew 30 collars on 30 shirts in an hour. That's a shirt every two minutes. That's a collar every two minutes.

INTERVIEWER: How many other people are working in the same place as you?

WOMAN: There are 75 of us in this very crowded room. All of us sewing collars on shirts. There is not much room to move around. We must stay in our chairs. We must stay at our sewing machines. We work through the morning. At 12:00 the whistle blows. Then we can go down to the bathroom. Then we can go to the lunch room. We open our lunch bundles and eat our lunch. We eat our lunch in 10 minutes. Then we can talk or sing for 20 minutes. In 30 minutes it is all over. We must go back to our sewing machines. We must go back to sewing collars on shirts. We must go back to sewing 30 collars on 30 shirts every hour.

INTERVIEWER: That sounds like very exhausting work. It must be very tiring doing that kind of work all the time.

WOMAN: We are tired. We are hurting. We are sore. But this is all we can do. We can only sew collars on shirts. This is what we do. Day after day, this is what we do. I work for 74 hours every week sewing collars on shirts. For that 74 hours I am paid 14 dollars. I am paid 14 dollars for my week of work. I am paid 14 dollars for my week of sewing collars on shirts.

INTERVIEWER: Why don't the workers get together to force the management to improve the working conditions?

WOMAN: That would never work.

INTERVIEWER: Why not?

WOMAN: Because workers are so cheap to find. Everybody needs a job to feed their family, and there are more workers than there are jobs. So if a group of workers decided to ask for better working conditions, the bosses would just fire them and hire some new people.

INTERVIEWER: But that doesn't seem fair.

WOMAN: It's not fair, but it's all we have.

INTERVIEWER: Do you mean to tell me that if you asked for better conditions, you'd be out of a job?

WOMAN: That's right. And even more important, I probably wouldn't be able to find another job in this town. I'd have a black mark next to my name, and nobody would ever want to hire me.

INTERVIEWER: So you're stuck doing a job that you don't like and that has lousy working conditions?

WOMAN: That's right. We have to put up and shut up. There's no other way.

NARRATOR: Not only were men and women subjected to the repetitive work of factory life; so too were children. In fact, more than one-third of the entire work force in the late 1800s was composed of children. Children were hired by factories simply because they could be paid less for doing the same amount of work as an adult.

INTERVIEWER: Excuse me, can you tell me what you're doing here?

CHILD 1: [bored] I'm working in a cotton mill. I'm putting spools of thread on a large machine. I'm putting spools of thread on a large machine and then threading the machine. I'm working on big machines. I'm working on big machines that use spools of thread. I'm working on big machines that have many spools of thread and many places to thread the spools. All day long I put spools of thread in large machines. I don't know how many spools of thread I put on the machines. The machines are running all the time, and they use a lot of thread. The machines work fast, and so I must work fast. I must watch the entire machine because the machine has many, many spools of thread on it. The machine goes around and around and turns the thread into large pieces of cloth.

INTERVIEWER: That sounds like hard work. Don't you ever get a break?

CHILD 1: Much thread is needed for the large pieces of cloth. The machines go all the time. And all the time I must put new spools of thread on the machine. All the time I must thread the machine with the new spools. Over and over and over again I do the same thing.

INTERVIEWER: What about your working conditions in the factory? Can you tell us what kind of conditions you must endure?

CHILD 1: It is hot in the factory. It is very hot in the factory. I get hot when I work. I get very hot when I work. There are no windows to open in this large factory. We work in a very large room with no windows and lots of machines. I work for 10 hours all day long. Ten hours putting spools on thread on the machine. For 10 hours of work I am paid 10 cents. I am paid one cent for each hour I work.

INTERVIEWER: That doesn't sound like very much. Why don't you get another job?

CHILD 1: Jobs are cheap. Children are cheap. All the jobs for children pay very little. That's all there is.

INTERVIEWER: Why are you working in the first place? Why aren't you home with your family? Why aren't you in school?

CHILD 1: My whole family works. We all need to work in order to survive. If everyone didn't work, we wouldn't have a place to live and we wouldn't have food to eat. I don't go to school because if I went to school, then we would lose all the money that I bring in. And then we might be thrown into the street.

INTERVIEWER: It sounds like a tough life?

CHILD 1: Yeah. It's a tough life.

NARRATOR: Children worked long and hard in many factories and industries. Many families needed the money earned by children in order to survive. Thus, when children reached a certain age—perhaps as young as seven—they were sent off to work and earn money for the family. Their lives were hard, and so were the working conditions.

INTERVIEWER: Can you tell us about what you do?

CHILD 2: [sadly] I work in a mine. Every day I work in a mine. I come to the mine at 6:00 in the morning. I don't leave the mine until 6:00 at night. I work

193

inside the mine for 12 hours every day. Every day I go into the mine and push out a coal car filled with coal. Two of us are assigned to a coal car, and we must push it out of the mine to the top. I am nine years old and I am strong, and I spend all day long pushing coal cars to the top of the mine. The work is hard and the work is long. All day I am in the darkness of the mine pushing coal cars.

INTERVIEWER: That sounds like dangerous work.

CHILD 2: Yes, the work is dangerous. My friend Billy had the fingers of his hand crushed by a coal car. There was no doctor. The other miners put a bandage around his hand and told him to work some more. His hand hurt, but he had to work. That was two weeks ago, and now his hand doesn't work anymore. All the bones were crushed in his hand, and now his hand does not work any more. But he still works in the mine. He still must work in the mine. He was a lucky one.

INTERVIEWER: What do you mean, he was a lucky one?

CHILD 2: Dolly used to work putting coal into the coal cars. She would pick up coal from the floor of the mine and put it into the coal cars. All day long that's what she did. One day she wasn't paying attention. One day a coal car was still moving along the track. Dolly wasn't looking. She had her foot on the track. The coal car ran over her foot. They put a bandage over her foot, but it was too late. Dolly lost some toes on her foot. Dolly lost some toes on her left foot. Dolly doesn't work here any more. She can't walk right. She can't work in the mines.

INTERVIEWER: What happened to her?

CHILD 2: I heard that she is now working in a factory in another town. I think the factory is a sewing factory. I think they make shirts. Dolly can sit down and make shirts all day long. Maybe she is lucky after

194

all. She can just sit down and make shirts all day long.

NARRATOR: The Industrial Revolution was a time of change, a time of change for individuals and a time of change for the country. It meant the mechanization of American society. It meant more machines doing more work. And it meant more jobs.

But it also meant lots of change. People were needed to run the machines, and labor was cheap. The owners of many factories knew that for every worker hired, there were more to replace that individual if he or she didn't work out. There was talk of forming labor unions to fight for the rights of workers, but in the early days of the Industrial Revolution it was just talk. The factory owners had all the power, and there was little that the workers could do. Nevertheless, these events set the stage for the eventual rise of labor unions. In many ways, these labor unions—organizations that fought for the rights of workers—became the inevitable outcome of the entire Industrial Revolution. It could be safely said, that for better or worse, the Industrial Revolution would have a major impact on American society for years to come.

Adapted from Anthony D. Fredericks, *Readers Theatre for American History* (Westport, CT: Teacher Ideas Press, 2001).

Day of the Wave

NOTE: This script is based on the book *The Tsunami Quilt: Grandfather's Story* by Anthony D. Fredericks. It illustrates how a single book can be used to develop an accompanying readers theatre script. Both teachers and librarians will find numerous opportunities to develop readers theatre scripts from other examples of children's literature.

STAGING: The narrator should be placed off to the side and in front of the other actors. The actors should be seated on stools or chairs.

		Pua X		Ulani X		
	Noa X					Kimo X
Narrator X						

NARRATOR: One of the ancient traditions of native Hawaiians is "talking story." It is one way Hawaiians preserve and share their history. More than just a factual history, it is often personal recollections of the members of a specific family, the funny anecdotes, humorous stories, and fond reminiscences about relatives that are shared during family gatherings. Because Hawai'i is such a cultural melting pot, "talking story" is also a way of preserving qualities from each culture while blending them into a composite story. "Talking story" is similar to the conversations friends might have at a party.

NOA: So, Kimo, I understand that your grandfather was a very special person. You say that he was a big influence in your life.

KIMO: Yes, my grandfather was my all-time best friend. He always took me fishing down at the ocean. We would sometimes take long walks along the shore. But maybe the best times we had were when he told me stories.

PUA: What kind of stories did he tell you?

KIMO: He liked telling fishing stories the best. He had been a fisherman all his life, and he used to tell fish tales whenever he could. Of course, as a fisherman, he was known to stretch the truth now and again. But, that was okay, I still liked to hear him tell stories—especially the stories of long ago.

ULANI: Your grandfather sounds like a real neat guy. He must have had a lot of stories.

KIMO: Yes, but I think it was when he and I went down to Laupāhoehoe every spring that I remember the most.

NARRATOR: Laupāhoehoe (LAH-pah-hoy-hoy) is a small peninsula that juts out from the northern coast of the big island of Hawai'i. It was formed by an eruption of Mauna Loa many thousands of years ago.

KIMO: Each spring my grandfather and I would walk along the shore. We never said much on those special visits. But each time my grandfather would walk over to a marble monument, lay his hands on the top, and look out over the sea.

NOA: Did he say anything to you.

KIMO: No, this was the only time in his life that I ever saw him so quiet.

PUA: Then, what?

KIMO: He said that one day he would tell me a story about this special place. He said the place was one of remembrance and also one of tragedy.

ULANI: What did he mean by that?

KIMO: I didn't know at the time. It wasn't until after my grandfather died that I learned what he meant.

NOA: What did he mean? What did he mean by a place of remembrance?

KIMO: Well, it was actually my father who told me the story. He said that many, many years ago there was a school at Laupāhoehoe. One day, all the kids were getting off the bus when they saw something happening to the ocean water.

PUA: What was happening?

KIMO: The water was moving away from the shore. There were lots of fish flapping on the sand.

ULANI: I think I know what's going to happen.

KIMO: Yes, there was a tsunami coming. Before anyone knew what happened, the waves of the tsunami rolled onto the land. They were big. They were fierce. They swept everything around like in a giant washing machine.

NARRATOR: A tsunami can race across an open ocean at 500 miles per hour. When a tsunami nears shore, it slows down very quickly and the water beneath the wave piles up. In a brief moment, a 2-foot high wave at sea may be transformed into a 30-foot high wave on the shore. Typically, there are several waves in a row—a tsunami wave train.

NOA: Was your grandfather there?

KIMO: Yes, he was. And so was his little brother. But he didn't know where his little brother was. My grandfather was on some high ground, and as soon as he saw the tsunami hit he ran uphill as fast as he could go. But he didn't know where his brother was.

PUA: And then what happened, Kimo?

KIMO: My grandfather kept running and running uphill. All he could hear were people crying. Children and adults were screaming and crying. It was awful, he said.

ULANI: Did a lot of people die?

KIMO: Yes, when it was over 24 people had died. Students and teachers had all been caught in the power of the tsunami. It was terrible.

NOA: Don't tell me! Don't tell me!

KIMO: Yes, one of the people who was killed that day was my grandfather's little brother. He felt helpless, because there was nothing he could do to save him. He was gone forever.

PUA: So is that why he went to Laupāhoehoe every year?

KIMO: Yes, he wanted to honor the memory of his little brother. He wanted to remember his little brother in a special way.

ULANI: That is a sad story . . . a very sad story.

KIMO: Yes, and it is a story we should never forget. Because as my grandfather used to say, "The ocean gives, but it also takes."

NOA: What else, Kimo?

KIMO: Well, there is something else. But I cannot tell you. It is something you must see for yourself.

PUA: What is it?

KIMO: You must go to The Pacific Tsunami Museum in Hilo to see it for yourself. When you see it you will never be the same. It is something very special. It is

199

something you will always remember. It will touch you in a very magical way.

ULANI: What is it?

NARRATOR: It is "The Tsunami Quilt." But that is something for another story and another time. In the meantime, perhaps you will read the children's book about that story and about that time. The book is called *The Tsunami Quilt: Grandfather's Story*. It, too, is a story to remember.

Humorous Adaptations

Beauty and This Incredibly Ugly Guy

STAGING: Narrator 1 may stand to the left of the staging area; Narrator 2 may stand to the right. The two characters may be seated on high stools or chairs in the center. They may wish to use plastic toy phones as props.

	Ugly Guy X	Beauty X	
Narrator 1 X			Narrator 2 X

NARRATOR 1: [rambling and rapid] Once upon a time there was this deep dark forest in which there was a little cottage where this man and this woman lived with all their children and all the animals of the forest would be their friends and they ate berries and leaves and everyone was happy and smiling and just wanted to be left alone so they could eventually live happily ever after except for the fact that these out-of-work storytellers came wandering through the forest one day and decided to turn the family's

life into some incredibly neat fairy tale or fable or legend or something like that so that they would all become incredibly rich and be able to live happily ever after for the rest of their lives, but do you think they even thought of sharing all their riches with that family deep in the enchanted forest? No, of course they didn't; but that's probably another story which I don't have time to tell you because I'm trying to tell you this story that really isn't a real story but just a story I made up because I wanted to get rich and famous like all those other storytellers so what I did was take one of their stories—actually I just borrowed it for a while—and decided to change just a couple of the facts and events, well, maybe I changed a lot of the facts and events, so that I could tell it to you all and you all would become incredibly excited and want to hear it again and again and want to tell your friends about this story and they would want to hear it again and again and, of course, I would become very rich and very famous and invite you all over to my castle and give you a ride in my incredibly fast carriage, but maybe I'm getting ahead of myself, perhaps I'd better just tell you the story and see if you like it first—okay? okay? okay?—well, anyway, here goes!

[slower] Once upon a time there was this really gorgeous looking blond maiden; I mean a real knock-out, a real beauty, with a fantastic personality and everything. As you might expect, all the princes from the local castle wanted to date her and take her to the movies, and concerts, and all the other kinds of things guys do with incredibly beautiful maidens. But this incredibly ravishing young maiden didn't like all the young men in the castle, most of whom were about as stupid as a doormat anyway. Well, it just so happened that there was this really ugly guy over in the next castle. I mean, you talk about ugly; he was so bad he made paint peel just by being in a room. He was so ugly he had to put a bag over his

203

head just to sneak up on a glass of water to take a drink. He was so ugly that dogs would howl whenever he walked by. He was so ugly . . . .

NARRATOR 2: Will you just get on with the story, already?

NARRATOR 1: Okay, okay. So anyway, this really, really, really ugly guy wants to take the fantastically stunning young maiden out for a date. So he calls her up one evening.

UGLY GUY: Good evening, may I please speak to the phenomenally stunning young maiden, please. Thank you. [pause] Hello, wonderfully gorgeous young maiden. This is the incredibly ugly guy.

BEAUTY: Oh, hello. Don't you sit behind me in math class?

UGLY GUY: Yeah, that's me. I thought you never noticed me.

BEAUTY: Well, actually, I haven't. It's just that all the other girls have been talkin' about you. So what do you want?

UGLY GUY: [shyly] Wel-l-l-l-l-l-l-l-l. You see. The Fall Ball is coming up in a few weeks down at the castle. And I was just sorta, kinda, well you see I was just thinking and wondering and maybe even kinda hopin' that . . . well, would you like to go with me to the ball.

BEAUTY: Are you asking me for a date?

UGLY GUY: [unsure and rambling] Well, yes I am. Would you like to go with me? I mean I realize that I'm certainly one of the ugliest and strangest and most repulsive creatures you've ever seen. And I'm probably not a very good dancer or anything like that. And I can barely carry on a conversation with anyone. And sometimes I have bad breath and really gross people out when I talk with them. And I'm sorta clumsy and will probably spill punch and cookies all over you. And I never take a bath and probably smell like I've been living in a sewer all my life. And I never comb my hair or brush my teeth. And my clothes are all dirty and torn and beat up and ragged and stained and all that stuff. And I never clip my toenails or wash my socks. But in spite of all that, I've got a really great personality.

BEAUTY: Well, you know, I am sort of intrigued. I've never really gone out with an extraordinarily grotesque and hideous guy before. It sounds like it might be fun. Okay, yeah, sure, why not? Let's go out.

UGLY GUY: [excited] Oh, wow! That's great. Look, why don't I pick you up in my beat up old hay wagon next Friday night at about 7:00. Okay?

BEAUTY: That sounds good. I'll see you then.

NARRATOR 2: And so it was that this remarkably repulsive and unattractive guy was able to take the most incredibly ravishing and stunning maiden in the whole kingdom to the annual Fall Ball. And, of course, they had a great time . . . except for that time the really monstrous and unsightly guy tried to kiss the wonderfully and exquisitely beautiful young maiden. But that's another story.

Adapted from Anthony D. Fredericks, *Frantic Frogs and Other Frankly Fractured Folktales for Readers Theatre* (Westport, CT: Teacher Ideas Press, 1993).

Don't Kiss Sleeping Beauty, She's Got Really Bad Breath

STAGING: The narrator stands off to the side. The characters may each sit on a separate stool or chair. They may wish to stand in a circle in front of the audience, too.

Narrator				
X				
	Prince 1	Prince 2	Prince 3	Prince 4
	X	X	X	X

NARRATOR: Once upon a time, there was this very beautiful princess. All the princes wanted to marry her. However, one day a wicked witch made this beautiful girl eat a poisoned apple. Beauty (that was her name) fell fast asleep. All the princes knew that it would take a kiss to wake her up.

PRINCE 1: Wow! All I have to do is kiss Sleeping Beauty and she will awaken from her sleep to be my bride.

NARRATOR: [to the prince] That's right, Prince 1.

NARRATOR: [to the audience] Let's see what happens when Prince 1 returns to the castle to tell his prince friends about his discovery.

PRINCE 1: Hey, guys. You're not going to believe this, but Sleeping Beauty is sound asleep in the enchanted forest. And she is waiting for one of us to give her a kiss that will wake her up.

PRINCE 2: Well, why didn't you kiss her?

PRINCE 1: Well, it seems as she has really bad breath. . . . I mean really bad breath! WHEW! Did it stink!!!

PRINCE 3: You mean, you didn't kiss her after all?

PRINCE 1: No way, José. Her breath was so bad, I couldn't even get in the room.

PRINCE 4: That's hard to believe. You mean, her breath is so bad that we can't even get close enough to kiss her? Wow, what a waste!

PRINCE 1: Yeah and you know what else? She snores like a bear. Every time she breathes the windows rattle and the dishes in the kitchen crack and break.

PRINCE 3: Boy, that's unbelievable!

PRINCE 1: Not only is she stinking up the air, but she's making the whole neighborhood shake with her snoring. Nobody wants to live in the enchanted forest anymore.

PRINCE 2: Well, how are we going to wake her up? Doesn't somebody have to kiss her in order for this story to end the right way?

PRINCE 1: Hey, maybe you pal, but not me! If you want to go ahead and kiss old "Hog's Breath," then help yourself.

NARRATOR: And so nobody wanted to kiss Sleeping Beauty. She just slept in the forest making loud noises and stinking up the air. And if you ever go into the forest and listen real hard, you can still hear her today.

_____

Adapted from Anthony D. Fredericks, *Frantic Frogs and Other Frankly Fractured Folktales for Readers Theatre* (Westport, CT: Teacher Ideas Press, 1993).

The Boy Who Cried "Amphibian"

(Once Too Often, I Might Add)

STAGING: Narrator 1 may be seated on a tall stool to the left of the staging area; Narrator 2 may be seated on a tall stool to the right. The other characters should be standing and walking around the staging area.

Narrator 1				Narrator 2
X				X
	Villager 1	Villager 2	Villager 3	
	X	X	X	
Boy				
X				

NARRATOR 1:   Once upon a time in a small village in a small country there was a shepherd boy.

NARRATOR 2: Now, we should point out that a shepherd boy is a boy who takes care of shepherds.

NARRATOR 1: No, he's not, silly. A shepherd boy is a young boy who is given the job of watching over a herd of sheep.

NARRATOR 2: I've heard of sheep!

NARRATOR 1: Not that kind of "heard." A herd of sheep is a whole bunch of sheep all in one place.

NARRATOR 2: Oh, I get it!

NARRATOR 1: Anyway, as I was saying . . . there was this shepherd boy in a small village in a small country a long time ago.

NARRATOR 2: Hey, maybe I might want to be a shepherd some day. You know, after this narrator gig I might want another job. How much money does a shepherd make?

NARRATOR 1: [getting frustrated] I don't know, and I don't care! Besides, it has nothing to do with the story we're trying to tell.

NARRATOR 2: Oh, okay. Then go ahead.

NARRATOR 1: Anyway, as I was saying . . . there was this shepherd boy and he was asked to take care of the village flock. That is, his job was to take care of all the sheep that belonged to the village.

NARRATOR 2: Hey, what's a flock? Can I buy one at the store?

NARRATOR 1: No, you can't. A flock is like a group or a whole bunch of something.

NARRATOR 2: Oh, like a whole flock of kids on the playground?

NARRATOR 1: No, you can't have a flock of students. You can only have a flock of animals, like sheep.

NARRATOR 2: Oh, I get it!

NARRATOR 1: I hope you do!

NARRATOR 2: So, there he was one day just sitting around watching these stupid sheep . . . .

NARRATOR 1: Hey, look, sheep aren't stupid, they just don't do very much except chew grass and mess up the lawn.

NARRATOR 2: So the little boy was sitting around—bored out of his skull—when he got a great idea. "I'll fool the villagers," he said, "because I'm really very bored and need something to amuse myself."

NARRATOR 1: So, he yelled . . . .

BOY: [loudly] Amphibians! Amphibians! Help! Help! Amphibians are chasing the sheep!!

NARRATOR 2: All the villagers heard the cries of the little shepherd boy and ran up the hill to help drive the amphibians away.

VILLAGER 1: Hey, little shepherd boy, didn't you just yell, "Amphibians?"

BOY: Yes, I did.

VILLAGER 2: Well, we just ran all the way up this hill only to find that there are no amphibians anywhere to be found.

VILLAGER 3: Yeah, the sheep are all quietly munching on their grass, and there are no amphibians anywhere. Were you kidding us?

BOY: Why, yes I was. It just gets so boring around here watching these stupid sheep . . . .

NARRATOR 1: Now, wait a minute. Like I said before, sheep aren't stupid. So, maybe they can't do three-column subtraction, but that doesn't mean they're dumb.

BOY: Anyway, it's really boring here.

NARRATOR 2: Well, all the villagers were really ticked off at the little shepherd boy for fooling them like that. And they all went back down the hill to the village, where they were all watching the latest episode of *American Idol*.

211

NARRATOR 1: Hey, wait a minute. This story takes place a long time ago . . . a long time ago before televisions were even invented.

NARRATOR 2: Oh, okay. Maybe they just went back to the village and sat around watching grass grow.

NARRATOR 1: Well, the boy was still back on the hill watching his sheep. And getting even more bored. So, he decided to have some more fun and he yelled . . .

BOY: Amphibians! Amphibians!! The amphibians are coming to get the sheep!!!

NARRATOR 2: I bet I know what happened.

NARRATOR 1: That's right. All the villagers ran up the hill to see what all the commotion was about.

NARRATOR 2: Yeah, 'cause they didn't want those big old hairy amphibians messing around with their cute little sheep.

NARRATOR 1: Hey, amphibians aren't hairy.

NARRATOR 2: [amazed] Oh. Okay.

NARRATOR 1: So the villagers ran up the hill. But when they got to the top they just saw the little shepherd boy, laughing away.

BOY: Ha, ha, ha!

VILLAGER 1: Hey, little shepherd boy. Did you fool us again by yelling "amphibians" when there were no amphibians at all?

BOY: Yes, I did.

VILLAGER 2: You know, that isn't very nice.

BOY: Yes, but it's so gosh darn boring up here with these sheep, I just wanted something to do.

VILLAGER 3: Well, perhaps you can find a game or something. We're getting sick and tired of your stupid pranks.

We can't keep running up here every time you yell something.

VILLAGER 1: You should save your yelling for when there is something really wrong.

VILLAGER 2: Don't cry "Amphibians!" when there are no amphibians!

VILLAGER 3: [pointing to Villager 2] Yeah, what he said.

NARRATOR 1: With that, all the villagers climbed back down the hill once again. They were all pretty ticked at the little shepherd boy.

NARRATOR 2: I bet I can guess what happened next.

NARRATOR 1: You're probably right. The little shepherd boy saw a real amphibian prowling about his flock of sheep. Alarmed, he leaped to his feet and yelled as loudly as he could . . .

BOY: AMPHIBIAN! AMPHIBIAN!!

NARRATOR 2: I bet the villagers thought that he was trying to fool them again.

NARRATOR 1: You're right. They thought he was fooling them again. So they didn't do anything. They waited . . . and waited . . . and waited. But at sunset, everybody wondered why the little shepherd boy hadn't returned to the village with all the sheep.

VILLAGER 1: Where's that little shepherd boy?

VILLAGER 2: Where's our sheep?

VILLAGER 3: Let's go see.

NARRATOR 2: So, what did they discover?

NARRATOR 1: The villagers went up the hill. There was the little shepherd boy, but all the sheep were gone.

BOY: There really was a big hairy amphibian here. He came and ate all the sheep. Now all the sheep are gone. I yelled "Amphibian." Why didn't you come?

213

VILLAGER 1: We thought you were fooling us again.

VILLAGERS 2 & 3: [pointing to Villager 1]Yeah, what he said.

NARRATOR 1: So it was that the village lost all its sheep to the big hairy amphibian.

NARRATOR 2: And I bet that there's a moral to this story, right?

NARRATOR 1: Right! The moral is, "Never get the villagers *hopping* mad, or all your sheep may *croak*!" Get it? "Never get the villagers HOPPING mad, or [slowly] . . . all . . . your . . . sheep . . . may . . . CROAK!"

Adapted from Anthony D. Fredericks, *More Frantic Frogs and Other Frankly Fractured Folktales for Readers Theatre* (Westport, CT: Teacher Ideas Press, 2008).

References

Allington, R. L. 1983. "Fluency: The Neglected Reading Goal." *The Reading Teacher* 36: 556–61.

Blevins, W. 2001. *Building Fluency: Lessons and Strategies for Reading Success*. New York: Scholastic.

Bloom, B. J., et al. 1956. *Taxonomy of Educational Objectives Handbook I: Cognitive Domain*. New York: David McKay.

Cohen, D. 1968. "The Effect of Literature on Vocabulary and Comprehension." *Elementary English* 45: 209–13, 217.

Cunningham, A. E., and K. E. Stanovich. 1998. "What Reading Does for the Mind." *American Educator* 22: 8–15.

Cunningham, P., and R. Allington. 2003. *Classrooms That Work: They Can All Read and Write*. Boston: Allyn & Bacon.

Dixon, N., A. Davies, and C. Politano. 1996. *Learning with Readers Theatre: Building Connections*. Winnipeg, MB: Peguis Publishers.

Dowhower, S. L. 1989. "Repeated Reading: Research into Practice." *The Reading Teacher* 42: 502–7.

Duffy, G., and J. Hoffman. 1999. "In Pursuit of an Illusion: The Flawed Search for a Perfect Method." *The Reading Teacher* 53: 10–16.

Fredericks, A. D. 1993. *Frantic Frogs and Other Frankly Fractured Folktales for Readers Theatre*. Westport, CT: Teacher Ideas Press.

———. 2001. *Guided Reading for Grades 3–6*. Austin, TX: Harcourt Achieve.

———. 2007. *Nonfiction Readers Theatre for Beginning Readers*. Westport, CT: Teacher Ideas Press.

———. 2008a. *MORE Frantic Frogs and Other Frankly Fractured Folktales for Readers Theatre*. Westport, CT: Teacher Ideas Press.

———. 2008b. *African Legends, Myths, and Folktales for Readers Theatre*. Westport, CT: Teacher Ideas Press.

Freppon, P., and K. Dahl. 1998. "Theory and Research Into Practice: Balanced Instruction: Insights and Considerations." *Reading Research Quarterly* 33: 240–51.

Garrison, J. 1997. *Dewey and Eros: Wisdom and Desire in the Art of Teaching*. New York: Teachers College Press.

Harris, T., and R. Hodges, eds. 1995. *The Literacy Dictionary: The Vocabulary of Reading and Writing*. Newark, DE: International Reading Association.

Koskinen, P. S., and I. H. Blum. 1986. "Paired Repeated Reading: A Classroom Strategy for Developing Fluent Reading." *The Reading Teacher* 40: 70–75.

Martinez, M., and N. Roser. 1985. "Read It Again: The Value of Repeated Readings During Storytime." *The Reading Teacher* 38: 782–86.

Martinez, M., N. Roser, and S. Strecker. 1999. " 'I Never Thought I Could Be a Star': A Readers Theatre Ticket to Reading Fluency." *The Reading Teacher* 52: 326–34.

Meinbach, A. M., A. D. Fredericks, and L. Rothlein. 2000. *The Complete Guide to Thematic Units: Creating the Integrated Curriculum.* Norwood, MA: Christopher-Gordon Publishers.

Morgan, R., and E. Lyon. 1979. "Paired Reading—A Preliminary Report on a Technique for Parental Tuition or Reading—Retarded Children." *Journal of Child Psychology and Psychiatry* 20: 151–60.

National Assessment Governing Board. 2002. *Reading Framework for the 2003 National Assessment of Educational Progress.* Available at www.nagb.org/pubs/reading_framework/toc.html.

National Reading Panel. 2000. *Teaching Children to Read: An Evidence-Based Assessment of Scientific Research Literature on Reading and its Implications for Reading Instruction.* Bethesda, MD: National Institutes of Health.

Rasinski, T. V. 2003. *The Fluent Reader: Oral Reading Strategies for Building Word Recognition, Fluency, and Comprehension.* New York: Scholastic.

Routman, R. 2003. *Reading Essentials: The Specifics You Need to Teach Reading Well.* Portsmouth, NH: Heinemann.

Samuels, S. J. 1979. "The Method of Repeated Reading." *The Reading Teacher* 32: 403–8.

Sebesta, S. 2003. *The Art of Teaching.* Available at www.teachervision.com/tv/resources/specialist/ssebesta2.html.

Strecker, S. K., N. L. Roser, and M. G. Martinez. 1999. "Toward Understanding Oral Reading Fluency." *Yearbook of the National Reading Conference* 48: 295–310.

Strickland, D. 1995. "Reinventing Our Literacy Programs." *The Reading Teacher* 48: 294–302.

Tyler, B., and D. J. Chard. 2000. "Using Readers Theatre to Foster Fluency in Struggling Readers: A Twist on the Repeated Reading Strategy." *Reading and Writing Quarterly* 16: 163–8.

Weaver, C., ed. 1998. *Reconsidering a Balanced Approach to Reading.* Urbana, IL: National Council of Teachers of English.

Wiggens, G., and J. McTighe. 1998. *Understanding by Design.* Alexandria, VA: Association for Supervision and Curriculum Development.

Wiske, M. S., ed. 1998. *Teaching for Understanding.* San Francisco: Jossey-Bass.

Wolf, S. 1998. "The Flight of Reading: Shifts in Instruction, Orchestration, and Attitudes Through Classroom Theatre." *Reading Research Quarterly* 33: 382–415.

Worthy, J. 2005. *Readers Theatre for Building Fluency.* New York: Scholastic.

More Teacher Resources

by

Anthony D. Fredericks

The following books are available from Teacher Ideas Press (88 Post Road West, Westport, CT 06881); 1-800-225-5800; http://www.teacherideaspress.com.

African Legends, Myths, and Folktales for Readers Theatre. ISBN 978-1-59158-633-3. (166pp.; $25.00).

Teachers are continually looking for materials that will enhance the study of cultures around the world. This collection of readers theatre scripts offers just that through an approach to the cultural study of Africa that will be fun and motivational for students—and improve their reading fluency.

American Folklore, Legends, and Tall Tales for Readers Theatre. ISBN 978-1-59158-734-7. ($25.00).

This collection of more than 20 well-known tales ("John Henry," "Paul Bunyan," Johnny Appleseed") will be invaluable to teachers and librarians as they do their usual units of study in American history and American Literature in the elementary and middle grades. Plays focus on well-known tales while building appropriate fluency skills.

Frantic Frogs and Other Frankly Fractured Folktales for Readers Theatre. ISBN 1-56308-174-1 (124pp.; $19.50)

Have you heard "Don't Kiss Sleeping Beauty, She's Got Really Bad Breath" or "The Brussels Sprouts Man (The Gingerbread Man's Unbelievably Strange Cousin)"? This resource (grades 4–8) offers 30 reproducible satirical scripts for rip-roaring dramatics in any classroom or library.

The Integrated Curriculum: Books for Reluctant Readers, Grades 2-5 (2nd Edition). ISBN 0-87287-994-1. (220pp.; $22.50).

This book presents guidelines for motivating and using literature with reluctant readers. The book contains more than 40 book units on titles carefully selected to motivate the most reluctant readers.

Investigating Natural Disasters Through Children's Literature: An Integrated Approach. ISBN 1-56308-861-4. (194pp.; $28.00).

Tap into students' inherent awe of storms, volcanic eruptions, hurricanes, earthquakes, tornadoes, floods, avalanches, landslides, and tsunamis to open their minds to the wonders and power of the natural world. .

Involving Parents Through Children's Literature: P–K. ISBN 1-56308-022-2. (86pp.; $15.00).

Involving Parents Through Children's Literature: Grades 1–2. ISBN 1-56308-012-5. (96pp.; $14.50).

Involving Parents Through Children's Literature: Grades 3–4. ISBN 1-56308-013-3. (96pp.; $15.50).

Involving Parents Through Children's Literature: Grades 5–6. ISBN 1-56308-014-1. (108pp.; $16.00)

This series of four books offers engaging activities for adults and children that stimulate comprehension and promote reading enjoyment. Reproducible activity sheets based on high-quality children's books are designed in a convenient format so that children can take them home.

The Librarian's Complete Guide to Involving Parents Through Children's Literature: Grades K–6. ISBN 1-56308-538-0. (138pp.; $24.50).

Activities for 101 children's books are presented in a reproducible format, so librarians can distribute them to students to take home and share with parents.

MORE Frantic Frogs and Other Frankly Fractured Folktales for Readers Theatre. ISBN 978-1-59158-628-9. (166pp.; $25.00).

Remember all the fun you had with the original *Frantic Frogs*? Well, they're back!! Here's another laugh-fest overflowing with scripts that will leave students (and teachers) rolling in the aisles (Don't miss "The Original Hip-Hop [by Busta Frog]").

MORE Science Adventures with Children's Literature: Reading Comprehension and Inquiry-Based Science. ISBN 978-1-59158-619-7. (444pp.; $35.00).

Get ready for hundreds of hands-on, minds-on projects that will actively engage students in positive learning experiences. Each of the 62 units offers book summaries, science topic areas, critical thinking questions, classroom resources, reproducible pages, and lots of easy-to-do activities, including science experiments for every grade level.

MORE Social Studies Through Children's Literature: An Integrated Approach. ISBN 1-56308-761-8. (226pp.; $27.50).

Energize your social studies curriculum with dynamic, hands-on, minds-on projects based on such great children's books as *Amazing Grace*, *Fly Away Home*, and *Lon Po Po*. This book is filled with an array of activities and projects sure to "energize" any social studies curriculum.

Mother Goose Readers Theatre for Beginning Readers. ISBN 978-1-59158-500-8. (168pp.; $25.00).

Designed especially for educators in the primary grades, this resource provides engaging opportunities that capitalize on children's enjoyment of Mother Goose rhymes. There is lots to share and lots to enjoy in the pages of this resource.

MUCH MORE Social Studies Through Children's Literature: A Collaborative Approach. ISBN 978-1-59158-445-2. (278pp.; $35.00).

This collection of dynamic literature-based activities will help any teacher or librarian energize the entire social studies curriculum and implement national (and state) standards. This resource is filled with hundreds of hands-on, minds-on projects.

Nonfiction Readers Theatre for Beginning Readers. ISBN 978-1-59158-499-5. (220pp.; $25.00).

This collection of science and social studies nonfiction scripts for beginning readers is sure to "jazz up" any language arts program in grades 1–3. Teachers and librarians will discover a wealth of creative opportunities to enhance fluency, comprehension, and appreciate of nonfiction literature.

Readers Theatre for American History. ISBN 1-56308-860-6. (174pp.; $30.00).

This book offers a participatory approach to American history in which students become active in several historical events. These 24 scripts give students a "you are there" perspective on critical milestones and colorful moments that have shaped the American experience.

Science Adventures with Children's Literature: A Thematic Approach. ISBN 1-56308-417-1. (190pp.; $24.50).

Focusing on the National Science Education Standards, this activity-centered resource uses a wide variety of children's literature to integrate science across the elementary curriculum. With a thematic approach, it features the best in science trade books along with stimulating hands-on, minds on activities in all the sciences.

Science Discoveries on the Net: An Integrated Approach. ISBN 1-56308-823-1. (316pp.; $27.50)

This book is designed to help teachers integrate the Internet into their science programs and enhance the scientific discoveries of students. The 88 units emphasize key concepts—based on national and state standards—throughout the science curriculum.

Silly Salamanders and Other Slightly Stupid Stuff for Readers Theatre. ISBN 1-56308-825-8. (162pp.; $23.50).

The third entry in the "wild and wacky" readers theatre trilogy is just as crazy and just as weird as the first two. This unbelievable resource offers students in grades 3–6 dozens of silly send-ups of well-known fairy tales, legends, and original stories.

Social Studies Discoveries on the Net: An Integrated Approach. ISBN 1-56308-824-X. (276pp.; $26.00).

This book is designed to help teachers integrate the Internet into their social studies programs and enhance the classroom discoveries of students. The 75 units emphasize key concepts—based on national and state standards—throughout the social studies curriculum.

Social Studies Through Children's Literature: An Integrated Approach. ISBN 1-87287-970-4. (192pp.; $24.00).

Each of the 32 instructional units contained in this resource utilizes an activity-centered approach to elementary social studies, featuring children's picture books such as *Ox-Cart Man, In Coal Country,* and *Jambo Means Hello.*

Songs and Rhymes Readers Theatre for Beginning Readers. ISBN 978-1-59158-627-2. (154pp.; $25.00).

Bring music, song, and dance into your classroom language arts curriculum with this delightful collection of popular rhymes and ditties. Beginning readers will enjoy learning about familiar characters in this engaging collection of scripts.

Tadpole Tales and Other Totally Terrific Titles for Readers Theatre. ISBN 1-56308-547-X. (116pp.; $18.50)

A follow-up volume to the best selling *Frantic Frogs and Other Frankly Fractured Folktales for Readers Theatre,* this book provides primary level readers (grades 1–4) with a humorous assortment of wacky tales based on well-known Mother Goose rhymes. More than 30 scripts and dozens of extensions will keep students rolling in the aisles.

Index

About the Author

Anthony D. Fredericks (afredericks60@comcast.net). Tony's background includes more than 38 years of experience as a classroom teacher, reading specialist, curriculum coordinator, staff developer, professional storyteller, and college professor. He is a prolific author, having written more than 70 teacher resource books, including the enormously popular *More Frantic Frogs and Other Frankly Fractured Folktales for Readers Theatre*, the best-selling *Guided Reading in Grades 3–6*, the celebrated *Much More Social Studies Through Children's Literature*, and the dynamic *Readers Theatre for American History*.

In addition, he's authored more than three dozen award-winning children's books, including *The Tsunami Quilt: Grandfather's Story, Near One Cattail: Turtles, Logs and Leaping Frogs, Dinosaur Droppings, Animal Sharpshooters*, and *A Is for Anaconda: A Rainforest Alphabet Book*.

Tony currently teaches elementary methods courses in reading, language arts, science, social studies, and children's literature at York College in York, Pennsylvania. In addition, he is a popular and enthusiastic visiting children's author to elementary schools throughout North America, where he celebrates books, writing, and storytelling.